R

S

C

*Super*

# READY
# STEADY
# COOK

# READY
# STEADY
# COOK

BRIAN TURNER  *25*

ANTONY WORRALL *24*
THOMPSON

PHOTOGRAPHS BY
JULIET PIDDINGTON

**BBC BOOKS**

This book is published to accompany the television series *Ready Steady Cook*
which was first broadcast in Autumn 1994.
The series is produced by Bazal Productions.

Published by BBC Books, an imprint of BBC Worldwide Publishing.
BBC Worldwide Ltd, Woodlands, 80 Wood Lane, London W12 0TT

First published 1996
Format © Bazal Productions
Recipes © Antony Worrall Thompson and Brian Turner
The moral right of the authors has been asserted
Editor: Jane Middleton
Home Economist: Carol Tennant
ISBN 0 563 38733 5

Set in Futura
Designed by Louise Morley
Printed by Martins the Printers Ltd., Berwick-upon-Tweed
Bound by Hunter & Foulis Ltd., Edinburgh
Colour Separations by Radstock Reproductions Ltd., Midsomer Norton
Colour printing by Lawrence Allen Ltd., Weston-super-Mare
Cover printed by Clays Ltd., St Ives Plc

# CONTENTS

# **INTRODUCTION**

At last! The *Ready Steady Cook* book has arrived. If you have ever started one of our recipes, fired with enthusiasm after the show, only to find you can't remember quite how it finished, this is the book for you.

On *Ready Steady Cook* we give our chefs the ultimate culinary test. The budget is £5, the time limit is 20 minutes and, on top of all that, the ingredients are a complete surprise. Our contestants have chosen a combination of foods they love and it's the chef's job to invent a delicious recipe there and then.

These recipes make it possible for anyone to rustle up a gourmet dish. The book is full of new ideas (even the chefs surprise themselves sometimes) and it's guaranteed to inspire good and bad cooks alike.

The point is to have a go – cooking is fun and the eating is even better! You can knock up a fabulous dish in 20 minutes for a fiver. Honestly. Go on – give it a try.

x

Presenter, *Ready Steady Cook*

# A NOTE ON INGREDIENTS AND TECHNIQUES

Good-quality ingredients make all the difference to the taste of the finished dish. For best results, choose unsalted butter and extra virgin olive oil. Buy ripe, flavoursome tomatoes whenever possible and really fresh herbs. If a recipe specifies dried herbs, freeze-dried ones usually have the best flavour. For desserts, chocolate should contain at least 50 per cent cocoa solids – check the back of the packet.

---

Some of the recipes contain raw or lightly cooked eggs. Because of the slight risk of salmonella poisoning, these should be avoided by the sick, the elderly, the very young, and pregnant women. The chances of contamination are greatly reduced if you buy free-range eggs, preferably organic, from a reputable supplier.

---

Many of the recipes in this book include wine. Use a wine that you would enjoy drinking rather than cheap 'cooking' wine – if it's not worth drinking, it's not worth cooking with!

Two techniques favoured by the chefs on *Ready Steady Cook* are cooking on a ridged grill pan and stock or sauce reduction.

Ridged grill pans are made of cast iron and usually have a spout for pouring off the cooking juices. They are a very healthy way of cooking because the ridges keep the food raised above any fat that runs off. They also make attractive grill marks on food – to make a crisscross pattern, give the food a half-turn half-way through cooking each side. Use ridged grill pans for steaks, chops, fish or chunky slices of vegetables such as aubergines, courgettes or peppers.

Stocks and sauces can be reduced by cooking them over a high heat until some of the liquid has evaporated. This concentrates the flavour and produces a thicker consistency. Because the flavour becomes more intense, you need to make sure you are using really good ingredients to start with – and in an ideal world this means homemade stock. However, you can buy fresh chilled stocks in cartons in supermarkets nowadays, which come a very good second best. In an emergency, take a tip from the chefs on *Ready Steady Cook* and use a stock cube diluted in a mixture of water and wine.

Finally, *Ready Steady Cook* is all about putting together a delicious meal from whatever ingredients you have to hand. The recipes in this book are proof that some of the most memorable dishes are the ones that come about on the spur of the moment. So if you don't have a particular ingredient, follow the example of our chefs and improvise. Don't be afraid to get in the kitchen and *Ready Steady Cook*!

# VEGETARIAN DISHES

FUSILLI WITH AUBERGINE
AND TOMATO SAUCE – 10

PATRICIA'S FUNGHI TRICOLORI – 11

A VARIATION ON VIV'S
VARIOUS VEGETABLES – 12

JACKIE'S ITALIAN STALLION – 14

## ANTONY WORRALL THOMPSON

# FUSILLI WITH AUBERGINE AND TOMATO SAUCE

*See photograph*

**SERVES 2**

225 g (8 oz) fusilli
5 tablespoons olive oil
1 small or $\frac{1}{2}$ large aubergine, cut into slices
1 cm ($\frac{1}{2}$ inch) thick
1 garlic clove, chopped
$\frac{1}{2}$ teaspoon chilli powder, or to taste

225 g (8 oz) ripe plum tomatoes, skinned and diced
2 teaspoons balsamic vinegar
1 tablespoon chopped fresh basil
Salt and freshly ground black pepper
A few sprigs of basil, to garnish

Cook the pasta in a large pan of boiling salted water for about 8 minutes or until *al dente*.

Meanwhile, make the sauce. Heat 3 tablespoons of the olive oil in a large frying pan and add the aubergine slices. Fry over a medium-high heat until tender and brown on both sides, then remove from the pan and drain on kitchen paper. When cool enough to handle, cut each slice into quarters. Heat 1 tablespoon of the remaining oil in the pan, add the garlic and chilli and cook gently for 1 minute without letting the garlic brown. Stir in the tomatoes, balsamic vinegar and chopped basil and season with salt and pepper to taste. Stir in the aubergines and remove from the heat.

To serve, drain the pasta and toss with the remaining olive oil, then mix with the aubergine and tomato sauce. Garnish with sprigs of basil.

---

### READY STEADY COOK Tip

*If you have time, it is a good idea to salt the aubergine slices first to remove any bitter juices. Place them in a colander, sprinkle with salt and leave to drain for 30 minutes to 1 hour, then rinse and pat dry.*

---

## ANTONY WORRALL THOMPSON

# PATRICIA'S FUNGHI TRICOLORI

Mushrooms stuffed with spinach and ricotta on a
tomato and herb sauce
*See photograph*

Patricia Roberts, a farmer's wife from Shrewsbury, had never cooked with ricotta cheese.
Antony showed her how, and used it to make a delicious stuffing for some giant mushrooms.

| SERVES 2 | |
|---|---|
| 4 large open-cap mushrooms | 3 tablespoons dry white wine |
| 40 g (1½ oz) butter | 1 x 400 g (14 oz) tin of chopped tomatoes |
| 3 garlic cloves, chopped | 1 tablespoon chopped fresh parsley |
| 1 onion, finely chopped | 1 tablespoon chopped fresh basil |
| 2 bay leaves | 150 g (5 oz) Cheshire cheese, grated |
| ½ teaspoon dried oregano | 225 g (8 oz) young spinach leaves |
| ½ teaspoon dried thyme | 225 g (8 oz) ricotta cheese |
| 1 teaspoon chopped fresh rosemary | Salt and freshly ground black pepper |
| | A few basil leaves, to garnish |

Pre-heat the oven to gas mark 6, 200°C (400°F).

Peel the mushrooms and remove the stalks, then chop the stalks
finely and set aside. Divide 25 g (1 oz) of the butter between the
mushroom caps, season with salt and pepper and put in the oven for
5 minutes.

Heat the remaining butter in a frying pan, add the garlic, onion,
bay leaves, dried herbs and rosemary and cook gently for about 5
minutes, until the onion is softened. Remove half this mixture from the
pan and set aside. Add the chopped mushroom stalks, white wine
and tinned tomatoes to the pan and simmer for about 10 minutes,
until slightly thickened. Stir in the parsley and basil and cook for a
further 3–4 minutes, then add half the grated cheese and season with
pepper to taste.

Wash the spinach, discarding any large stalks, then place it in a pan with only the water clinging to the leaves and cook for about 2 minutes, until just wilted. Leave until cool enough to handle and then squeeze out as much liquid as you can. Blend the spinach, ricotta and reserved onion mixture in a food processor until smooth, then season to taste. Spoon into the mushroom caps and return them to the oven for 5–10 minutes to heat through.

Sprinkle with the remaining cheese and place under a hot grill until golden and bubbling.

To serve, pour the tomato and herb sauce on to 2 warmed serving plates, place the mushrooms on top and garnish with basil leaves.

ANTONY WORRALL THOMPSON

# A VARIATION ON VIV'S VARIOUS VEGETABLES

### Deep-fried vegetables with rice patties and two dips

Vivien McManus from Cardiff is vegetarian and has varied tastes. Her father was in the army, which gave her the opportunity to travel the world, sampling local ingredients. She brought along a selection of vegetables with the addition of peanut butter, which she hoped would prove the ultimate challenge for Antony.

**SERVES 2–3**

1 large sweet potato, peeled and cut into thin chips
100 g (4 oz) okra, sliced into 1 cm ($\frac{1}{2}$ inch) lengths
1 cauliflower, cut into bite-sized florets
Sunflower oil for deep-frying
Salt and freshly ground black pepper
Sprigs of coriander, to garnish

**FOR THE RICE PATTIES**

100 g (4 oz) long grain rice
1 vegetable stock cube
1 lemon grass stalk, bruised
1 fresh kaffir lime leaf, or a strip of lime zest
$\frac{1}{4}$ fresh red chilli
1 tablespoon plain flour
1 egg, beaten
1 tablespoon sunflower oil
2 tablespoons smooth peanut butter

**FOR THE PEANUT DIP**
4 tablespoons smooth peanut butter
3 tablespoons double cream
2 teaspoons finely chopped onion
$3/4$ fresh red chilli, deseeded
and finely chopped
Juice of $1/2$–1 lime, to taste
2 tablespoons chopped fresh coriander

**FOR THE YOGHURT DIP**
150 ml (5 fl oz) Greek yoghurt
2 teaspoons finely chopped onion
1 garlic clove, crushed
2 tablespoons chopped fresh mint

First cook the rice for the patties. Bring a pan of water to the boil, add the stock cube, lemon grass, kaffir lime leaf or lime zest and red chilli, then stir in the rice. Simmer for 10–12 minutes, until the rice is tender, then drain and leave to cool.

Next make the dips. Mix together all the ingredients for each one, adding seasoning to taste, then transfer to a small serving bowl and set aside. The peanut dip should be quite thick but if it is too stiff, stir in a little water.

Blanch the sweet potato chips in a pan of boiling water for 1 minute, then drain well and dry on kitchen paper.

Remove the lemon grass, lime and chilli from the cooled rice, then stir in the flour, beaten egg and seasoning to taste. Heat the oil in a large frying pan over a moderately high heat and spoon in the rice mixture in 6 portions. Flatten slightly with the back of the spoon, make a small indentation in the centre of each patty and spoon in 1 teaspoon of the peanut butter, covering it with a little of the rice from the edges. Cook for 5 minutes, turning once, until the patties are crisp and golden brown. Keep warm.

Heat the oil for deep-frying in a saucepan or deep-fryer and fry the okra, sweet potato chips and three quarters of the cauliflower florets. Cook them in separate batches for about 3 minutes each, until golden and tender, taking care not to overcrowd the pan. Drain on kitchen paper and sprinkle with salt.

To serve, arrange the deep-fried vegetables, rice patties and raw cauliflower on a serving platter and garnish with sprigs of coriander. Serve with the peanut and yoghurt dips.

## ANTONY WORRALL THOMPSON

# JACKIE'S ITALIAN STALLION

### Bruschetta with olive paste, aubergine and Mozzarella
*See photograph*

Jackie Parrott from Hertfordshire is passionate about Italian food. She brought along her favourite ingredients and helped her favourite chef of all time cook this delicious recipe.

**SERVES 2**

4 tablespoons olive oil

2 large slices of white country-style bread, about 1 cm ($1/2$ inch) thick, crusts removed

1 garlic clove, cut in half

1 small or $1/2$ large aubergine, cut into slices 1 cm ($1/2$ inch) thick

1 x 100 g (4 oz) Mozzarella cheese in water (preferably buffalo Mozzarella), drained and sliced

Salt and freshly ground black pepper

**FOR THE OLIVE PASTE**

100 g (4 oz) black olives, pitted

1 garlic clove, chopped

$1^1/2$ tablespoons olive oil

2 tablespoons chopped fresh coriander

$1/2$ teaspoon Dijon mustard

1 teaspoon balsamic vinegar

**TO GARNISH**

1 large, ripe, flavoursome tomato, sliced

A few basil leaves

First make the olive paste by blending all the ingredients in a food processor until smooth. Taste and season with salt and pepper.

To make the bruschetta, heat 1 tablespoon of the olive oil in a frying pan, add the bread and fry until golden. Remove from the pan and rub with the cut garlic clove. Heat the remaining oil in the pan and fry the aubergine slices over a medium-high heat until golden on both sides. Remove from the pan and drain on kitchen paper.

Spread some of the olive paste on to the bruschetta, cover with the aubergine slices and arrange the Mozzarella on top. Place under a hot grill until the cheese begins to melt.

To serve, place the bruschetta on 2 plates and garnish with the tomato and leaves. Drizzle with olive oil and grind over some pepper.

# FISH DISHES

FISH AND CHIPS À LA WARRINGTON – 16

FILLETS OF PLAICE EN VERDURE – 17

MOULES EN VAPEUR AVEC
TOMATES FARCIES – 19

JIMINY SALMON FINOCCHIO – 20

DEBBIE'S HOLLY POTATO, SALMON
AND OTHER THINGS – 22

JULIE'S JERSEY SALMON ROYALE – 24

ANDI'S SOLE WITH A HEART – 25

SPICY MACKEREL FILLETS
ON TASTY TENBY TREATS – 27

JADE AND AMBER'S FLAME SURPRISE – 29

## BRIAN TURNER

# FISH AND CHIPS À LA WARRINGTON

Battered cod with deep-fried potato balls and cabbage parcels

*Karen Hawthorne from Warrington, Cheshire, hated fish – unless it came from a chippy. Brian converted her with a delicious dish of cod, prawns and potato balls*

**SERVES 2**

2 x 150–175 g (4–6 oz) cod fillets, skinned
2 tablespoons plain flour, seasoned
1 small egg
2 tablespoons double cream
1 tablespoon chopped fresh parsley
3 tablespoons sunflower oil
Salt and freshly ground black pepper

**FOR THE CABBAGE PARCELS**
100 g (4 oz) frozen peas
1 sprig of mint

4–6 green cabbage leaves
50 g (2 oz) butter
200 g (7 oz) small peeled prawns
2 tomatoes, chopped
1 tablespoon chopped fresh parsley

**FOR THE POTATO BALLS**
350 g (12 oz) potatoes, grated
$1/2$ small onion, grated
4 tablespoons self-raising flour
Sunflower oil for deep-frying

Pre-heat the oven to gas mark 4, 180°C (350°F).

First prepare the cabbage parcels. Bring a large pan of water to the boil and add the peas and mint. Place the cabbage leaves on top and cook for 3–4 minutes, removing the cabbage leaves after 2 minutes. Drain the peas. Heat half the butter in a frying pan, add the prawns, tomatoes, peas and parsley and cook gently for 4–5 minutes. Season to taste, then drain well and spoon the mixture into the centre of each cabbage leaf. Gather each leaf up into a parcel, wrap it in a tea towel and give it a firm wring. Unwrap the tea towel and take out the stuffed cabbage leaf, which should remain in a neat parcel. Place the cabbage parcels in a greased ovenproof dish, dot with the remaining butter and bake in the oven for 8–10 minutes.

Meanwhile, make the potato balls. Mix together the potatoes, onion and flour, season and shape into 12–14 small balls. Heat the sunflower oil in a saucepan or deep-fat fryer, drop in the potato balls and fry for 3 minutes or until golden. Remove with a slotted spoon and drain on kitchen paper. Keep warm.

Dust the cod with the seasoned flour, shaking off any excess. Make a batter by whisking together the egg, cream, parsley and seasoning. Dip the fish in the batter. Heat the oil in a frying pan and fry the fish over a medium heat for 3–5 minutes on each side.

To serve, place the fish on 2 warmed serving plates and surround with the cabbage parcels and potato balls.

## B R I A N   T U R N E R

# FILLETS OF PLAICE EN VERDURE

Rolled plaice fillets with spinach moulds and herb butter sauce
*See photograph*

Jenny Evans from Manchester loves fish but hates the bones. She brought along some plaice, potatoes and spinach, which Brian transformed into her dream meal.

| SERVES 2 | 1 large plaice, filleted and skinned |
|---|---|
| 100 g (4 oz) fresh spinach | 4 tablespoons dry white wine |
| 1 tablespoon olive oil | 400 ml (14 fl oz) fish or vegetable stock |
| 65 g (2½ oz) chilled butter | 3 tablespoons double cream |
| 1 small onion, finely diced | 2 tablespoons finely chopped fresh mixed |
| 2 garlic cloves, crushed | herbs, such as parsley, basil and tarragon |
| 1 large potato, finely diced | Salt and freshly ground black pepper |
| 3 tomatoes, skinned, de-seeded and chopped | |

Pre-heat the oven to gas mark 6, 200°C (400°F).

Wash the spinach, discarding any large stalks, then put it in a pan with only the water clinging to the leaves and cook for 2–3 minutes, until just wilted. Drain very thoroughly.

Heat the oil and 15 g ($^1/_2$ oz) of the butter in a frying pan and fry the onion, half the garlic and the potato for 10–15 minutes or until tender and golden brown. Add the tomatoes, reserving a few pieces for the sauce, and cook for 2 minutes. Season with salt and pepper to taste.

While the vegetables are cooking, place a spinach leaf on top of each plaice fillet, season, then roll up and fasten securely with a wooden cocktail stick. Place in a shallow casserole dish and pour over half the white wine and all except 3 tablespoons of the stock. Cook in the oven, uncovered, for about 5–6 minutes, until the fish is just done.

Meanwhile, line 2 greased 7.5 cm (3 inch) ramekin dishes or metal rings with the remaining spinach leaves, overlapping them and allowing the ends to overhang the edges of the containers. Fill with the tomato, onion and potato mixture, fold over the spinach to enclose the filling and bake in the oven for 10 minutes.

For the sauce, put the remaining wine and stock in a pan and boil until reduced to just under half its original volume. Add the remaining garlic and the reserved tomato pieces. Simmer for 2–3 minutes, then pass the sauce through a sieve into a clean pan and stir in the cream. Simmer for 3 minutes, then cut up the remaining butter and whisk it into the sauce a few pieces at a time until smooth. Stir in the chopped mixed herbs and season to taste.

To serve, place the fish rolls on 2 warmed serving plates and remove the cocktail sticks. Run a knife round the edge of the spinach moulds to loosen them and then turn them out and place next to the fish. Drizzle the sauce around the edges.

---

### READY STEADY COOK Tip
*Ask your fishmonger to fillet and skin the plaice (there should be 4 fillets) and to give you the trimmings to make the stock.*

---

## A N T O N Y   W O R R A L L   T H O M P S O N

# MOULES EN VAPEUR AVEC TOMATES FARCIES

Mussels steamed with coriander and lemon grass, served with stuffed tomatoes and lettuce chiffonade
*See photograph*

**Ben Mills runs a sandwich shop in Bristol and his dream meal is musssels, beer and chips. Antony obliged with a magnificent moules dish.**

**SERVES 2**
900 g (2 lb) mussels
1 Little Gem lettuce
40 g (1$^1$/$_2$ oz) butter
1 small onion, finely diced
2 garlic cloves, chopped
2 tablespoons chopped fresh coriander leaves
1 lemon grass stalk, finely chopped
$^1$/$_2$ teaspoon dried thyme
A pinch of chilli powder

120 ml (4 fl oz) dry white wine
salt and freshly ground black pepper

**FOR THE TOMATOES**
100 g (4 oz) fresh goat's cheese
$^1$/$_2$ small onion, very finely diced
3 anchovy fillets, chopped
1 tablespoon chopped fresh parsley
4 large tomatoes
15 g ($^1$/$_2$ oz) butter

Clean the mussels by scrubbing them thoroughly under cold running water and removing the beards. Cut the stalk out of the lettuce, reserve a few outer leaves and slice the rest into chiffonade (very fine strips).

For the tomatoes, mash together the goat's cheese, onion, anchovies and parsley, then season to taste. Slice the tops off the tomatoes and carefully scoop out the insides. Stuff with the goat's cheese mixture, put a knob of the butter on top of each one and place under a hot grill for 4–5 minutes, until heated through and lightly browned on top.

Meanwhile, cook the mussels. Melt 25 g (1 oz) of the butter in a pan, add the onion and garlic and cook gently for a few minutes until softened but not coloured. Stir in the coriander, lemon grass, thyme, chilli and wine, bring to the boil, then add the mussels. Cover and cook over a fairly high heat for 2–3 minutes, shaking the pan occasionally, until the shells have opened. Strain the mussels through a colander, reserving the liquid. Discard any mussels that remain closed. Pour the liquid into a pan and add the remaining butter. Simmer for a few minutes until slightly reduced, then stir in most of the lettuce chiffonade. Taste and adjust the seasoning.

To serve, open up the mussels and discard the top half of the shell, then arrange them around the edges of 2 heated serving plates. Place the reserved whole lettuce leaves in the centre and put the stuffed tomatoes on top, then pour the sauce over the mussels. Scatter over the remaining lettuce.

## ANTONY WORRALL THOMPSON

# JIMINY SALMON FINOCCHIO

Poached salmon with fennel, scallops, rice and watercress sauce

Jackie Orr from North London adores fish. She presented Antony with a luxurious selection of ingredients and he created this superb dish for her.

**SERVES 2**

100 g (4 oz) basmati rice
1 fennel bulb, cut into 6–8 wedges
450 ml (15 fl oz) vegetable stock
75 g (3 oz) watercress, leaves and stalks separated
2 x 175 g (6 oz) salmon steaks
40 g (1½ oz) butter
2 shallots, finely chopped
4 tablespoons dry white wine
1 small garlic clove, chopped
1 teaspoon chopped fresh thyme
1 bay leaf
150 ml (5 fl oz) double cream
A good squeeze of lemon juice
2 tablespoons olive oil
6 spring onions, chopped into 1 cm (½ inch) lengths
100 g (4 oz) scallops
1 teaspoon balsamic vinegar
Salt and freshly ground black pepper

Cook the rice in boiling salted water for 10–12 minutes, until just tender, then drain and keep warm. Cook the fennel in boiling salted water for about 6 minutes, until almost tender, then drain and set aside.

Pour the stock into a pan, add the watercress stalks and heat almost to boiling point. Season the salmon steaks and poach them in the stock for about 7 minutes, until just cooked. Remove from the pan, peel off the skin and keep the fish warm in a low oven. Leave the pan containing the stock on the heat and boil until reduced to a third of its original volume, then strain.

To make the sauce, melt 25 g (1 oz) of the butter in a small pan, add the shallots and sweat until softened. Add the white wine, garlic, thyme, bay leaf and reduced stock and simmer until the liquid has reduced to a third of its original volume. Stir in the cream and a good handful of the watercress leaves, then purée in a liquidizer until smooth. Return to the heat, add the lemon juice and simmer gently for 1–2 minutes. Taste and adjust the seasoning if necessary.

Heat the remaining butter and half the oil in a pan, add the spring onions and fennel and cook briskly for 5 minutes, until browned. Slice each scallop into 2 or 3 pieces, add to the pan and cook for between 30 seconds and 1 minute.

Mix together the balsamic vinegar, remaining olive oil and some salt to make a dressing. Pour on to the remaining watercress and toss well.

To serve, arrange the watercress salad on 2 warmed serving plates and place the salmon steaks on top. Spoon the rice to one side of the fish and the fennel and scallop mixture to the other. Pour the sauce around the edge.

---

**READY STEADY COOK Tip**
*Be careful not to overcook the scallops or they will be tough. They are done when opaque but slightly translucent in the centre.*

---

## BRIAN TURNER

# DEBBIE'S HOLLY POTATO, SALMON AND OTHER THINGS

Salmon and smoked trout parcels with potato pancakes, brandy cream sauce and watercress and orange salad

Deborah Barker's husband hates fish but she and her children love it. Brian created the ultimate treat, and Debbie contributed a festive decoration.

**SERVES 2**

75 g (3 oz) full-fat soft cheese
2 teaspoons yoghurt
1 tablespoon finely snipped fresh chives
175 g (6 oz) fresh salmon fillet, skinned and cut crosswise into 2.5 cm (1 inch) strips
100 g (4 oz) smoked trout fillet, cut lengthwise into 2.5 cm (1 inch) strips
150 ml (5 fl oz) fish or vegetable stock
4 tablespoons dry white wine
5 tablespoons double cream
A dash of brandy
50 g (2 oz) chilled butter, diced
2 tablespoons chopped mixed fresh herbs
Salt and freshly ground black pepper

**FOR THE POTATO PANCAKES**

275 g (10 oz) potatoes, diced
50 g (2 oz) plain flour
A pinch of salt
1 egg
120 ml (4 fl oz) milk
1 tablespoon olive oil

**FOR THE SALAD**

1 orange, peeled and divided into segments
1 bunch of watercress
2 tablespoons olive oil
2 teaspoons fresh orange juice

Pre-heat the oven to gas mark 6, 200°C (400°F).

To make the fish parcels, mix together the cream cheese, yoghurt and chives and season with salt and pepper. Lay each strip of salmon across the centre of a strip of smoked trout, spoon a little of the cream cheese mixture on top and fold the trout over to form a parcel. Place the fish parcels in a buttered shallow ovenproof dish. Put the stock and half the wine in a pan and bring to the boil, then pour it around the fish (it should come no more than half-way up the sides of the parcels). Cover with foil and bake in the oven for 8 minutes. Remove the fish parcels from the dish and keep warm; reserve the cooking liquid.

To make the pancakes, cook the potatoes in boiling salted water until tender, then drain and mash. Leave to cool. Whisk together the flour, salt, egg and milk, then add the mashed potato and whisk thoroughly until smooth. Heat the oil in a heavy-based frying pan. Pour in a couple of tablespoons of batter for each pancake and cook for about 3 minutes on each side or until golden brown. Keep warm.

For the sauce, put the remaining white wine in a pan and boil until reduced to about 1 tablespoon. Stir in the cream and brandy and simmer until reduced by half, then stir in 3 tablespoons of the reserved fish cooking liquid. Simmer until slightly reduced, then whisk in the butter a few pieces at a time until smooth. Stir in the mixed herbs and season to taste.

For the salad, arrange the orange segments on a bed of the watercress. Whisk together the oil and orange juice, season to taste and pour over the salad.

To serve, put the potato pancakes on 2 warmed serving plates and place the salmon and trout parcels on top. Pour the sauce over and accompany with the salad.

---

**READY STEADY COOK Tip**
*If it's Christmas, why not try making Debbie's holly potato garnish? Peel a large potato and cut it into slices about 5 mm (¹/₄ inch) thick. Cut them into holly shapes and fry in a little olive oil until crisp and golden.*

---

## BRIAN TURNER

# JULIE'S JERSEY SALMON ROYALE

Salmon with lemon butter, courgette ribbons and two salads

Julie Witt and her identical twin Jayne travelled from Jersey to challenge one another on *Ready Steady Cook*. Julie brought Brian some salmon and homegrown Jersey potatoes.

**SERVES 2**

2 small eggs, hard-boiled

3 tablespoons chopped fresh parsley

2 x 150–175 g (5–6 oz) salmon fillets, skinned

50 g (2 oz) butter

Juice of $\frac{1}{2}$ lemon

Salt and freshly ground black pepper

**FOR THE WARM POTATO SALAD**

225 g (8 oz) small new potatoes, preferably Jersey Royals

150 ml (5 fl oz) chicken stock

1 teaspoon grainy mustard

2 tablespoons mayonnaise

**FOR THE COURGETTE RIBBONS**

1 tablespoon olive oil

15 g ($\frac{1}{2}$ oz) butter

2 courgettes, sliced into ribbons with a vegetable peeler

**FOR THE MIXED SALAD**

3 tablespoons olive oil

1 tablespoon white wine vinegar

3 tomatoes, quartered

1 cucumber, diced

4 spring onions, sliced

A few lettuce leaves

First make the potato salad. Cook the potatoes in boiling salted water until tender, then drain. Pour the stock into a pan and boil until reduced to about 1 tablespoon. Stir in the mustard and mayonnaise and toss the potatoes in this dressing while still hot.

Push the hard-boiled eggs through a sieve, mix with the parsley and season well with salt and pepper. Coat one side of each salmon fillet (not the skin side) with this mixture, pressing it on firmly with your hands. Melt half the butter in a frying pan and fry the salmon, coated-side down, for 3 minutes. Turn and cook for another 3 minutes.

For the courgette ribbons, heat the olive oil and butter in a large frying pan, add the courgettes and toss over a medium heat for about 2 minutes, until just tender. Season to taste.

For the mixed salad, whisk together the olive oil and vinegar and season to taste. Arrange the tomatoes, cucumber and spring onions on a bed of lettuce leaves, pour over the dressing and toss lightly.

To serve, melt the remaining butter in a frying pan until just starting to sizzle, then remove from the heat and stir in the lemon juice. Put the courgette ribbons on 2 warmed serving plates and arrange the salmon fillets on top. Pour the lemon butter over the fish and serve the salads separately.

ANTONY WORRALL THOMPSON

# ANDI'S SOLE WITH A HEART

### Lemon sole with red pepper sauce, braised chicory, potatoes and guacamole

**Andi Theobald from Kettering, Northamptonshire, had just returned from a three-month trip to India and was pleased to get back to some home cooking! As an ex-dancer, she's keen on healthy eating and brought Antony a lemon sole in the hope of increasing her fish repertoire.**

**SERVES 2**

3 large potatoes
25 g (1 oz) butter
12 basil leaves
4 lemon sole fillets
1 tablespoon olive oil
Sunflower oil for deep-frying
Salt and freshly ground black pepper

**FOR THE GUACAMOLE**

1 avocado
1 tomato, finely chopped
2 tablespoons chopped fresh coriander
A pinch of chilli powder or cayenne pepper
1/4 red onion, finely chopped
Lime or lemon juice, to taste

**FOR THE CHICORY**

1 tablespoon olive oil
2 heads of chicory, sliced
A squeeze of lemon juice

**FOR THE RED PEPPER SAUCE**

1 red pepper, quartered and de-seeded
3 tablespoons double cream

Pre-heat the oven to gas mark 6, 200°C (400°F).

First make the guacamole. Peel and stone the avocado, then mash it with a fork. Stir in the remaining ingredients and season to taste with salt and pepper. Cover and set aside.

For the chicory, heat the olive oil in a small pan, then add the chicory and some salt and pepper. Cook for about 2 minutes, turning the chicory occasionally, then add the lemon juice, cover and cook for about 15 minutes, until very tender.

For the red pepper sauce, place the pepper quarters under a hot grill until charred and blistered. When cool enough to handle, peel off the skin and purée the pepper in a food processor or liquidizer. Add the cream and continue to process until smooth. Pour into a small pan, season to taste and reheat gently.

Peel and dice 2 of the potatoes and cook them in boiling salted water until tender. Drain and mash with the butter and seasoning to taste. Keep warm.

Lay 3 basil leaves on each lemon sole fillet, season and then roll up the fish with the basil leaves in the centre. Heat the olive oil in a shallow casserole dish or a small ovenproof frying pan and gently fry the fish on all sides for 2 minutes. Cover with a lid or aluminium foil and place in the oven for about 5 minutes to finish cooking.

Heat the oil for deep-frying in a saucepan or deep-fat fryer. Peel the remaining potato, then slice it as thinly as possible, using a vegetable peeler, a mandolin slicer or a very sharp knife. Pat the slices dry and then fry for 2–3 minutes, until golden brown. Drain the potato crisps on kitchen paper and sprinkle with salt.

To serve, pipe or spoon the mashed potato into the centre of a warmed serving platter. Remove the fish fillets from the pan with a fish slice to drain off the cooking juices and arrange them around the potato with the chicory. Pour the red pepper sauce over the fish and scatter over the potato crisps. Serve the guacamole separately.

---

**READY STEADY COOK Tip**
*You could serve the guacamole as a starter with tortilla chips.*

---

## B R I A N   T U R N E R

# SPICY MACKEREL FILLETS ON TASTY TENBY TREATS

*See photograph*

Trevayne Keohane from Tenby, West Wales, needed new ideas for cooking mackerel, as her nephew, a keen fisherman, often dumps them on her doorstep. Brian obliged with a delicious recipe using spinach and apple to complement the flavour of the fish.

**SERVES 4**

1 small loaf of white bread, preferably slightly stale
65 g (2¹/₂ oz) butter
1 tablespoon olive oil
2 tablespoons plain flour
¹/₂ teaspoon paprika
¹/₂ teaspoon cayenne pepper
¹/₂ teaspoon ground cumin
¹/₂ teaspoon garam masala
4 mackerel fillets
1 tablespoon chopped fresh parsley
Salt and freshly ground black pepper

**FOR THE APPLE AND SPINACH MIXTURE**

1 tablespoon olive oil
15 g (¹/₂ oz) butter
1 onion, diced
1 large cooking apple, peeled, cored and diced
175 g (6 oz) fresh spinach

**FOR THE PATTYPAN SQUASH MIXTURE**

1 tablespoon olive oil
175 g (6 oz) pattypan squash, diced
3 garlic cloves, crushed
4 tomatoes, cut into wedges

Pre-heat the oven to gas mark 6, 200°C (400°F).

Cut the loaf of bread horizontally in half and carefully cut out the centre from each half, leaving a thin shell. Cut half the bread into 2 cm (³/₄ inch) cubes (you don't need the rest of the soft bread for this recipe but you could make it into breadcrumbs for use in another dish; freeze them until required). Melt 25 g (1 oz) of the butter and brush it over the inside of the bread shells, then bake them in the oven for 6–8 minutes, until golden brown and crisp.

Heat the olive oil and 15 g ($^1/_2$ oz) of the remaining butter in a large frying pan and fry the bread cubes for about 4 minutes, until crunchy and golden brown. Set aside.

For the apple and spinach mixture, heat the oil and butter in a large pan, add the onion and cook gently for 5 minutes. Stir in the apple and cook for 5 minutes longer, until the apple is soft but still holds its shape.

Meanwhile, wash the spinach well, discarding any large stalks. Place in a large pan with just the water clinging to the leaves and cook for 3–4 minutes, until wilted.

Drain off any excess liquid and stir the spinach into the apple and onion mixture. Season to taste.

For the pattypan mixture, heat the oil in a pan and fry the squash for 5 minutes. Add the garlic and tomatoes, season and cook gently for about 5 minutes, until the squash is tender.

Next prepare the fish. Mix together the flour and spices. Coat the mackerel fillets with this mixture, shaking off any excess. Heat the remaining butter in a large frying pan and fry the fish over a medium-high heat for 2–3 minutes per side, until crisp on the outside and firm to the touch.

To serve, put the bread shells on a large serving plate, spoon the apple and spinach mixture into them and garnish with the croutons. Arrange the pattypan squash mixture around the bread shells and place the mackerel fillets on top. Sprinkle over the chopped parsley.

---

### READY STEADY COOK Tips

- *Pattypan squash are now stocked by most supermarkets in the summer months. They are members of the same family as courgettes. So if you cannot find them, you could substitute small, firm courgettes.*
- *If you are very short of time you could make this recipe without the bread, just serving the spicy fried mackerel with the two vegetable mixtures.*

A N T O N Y   W O R R A L L   T H O M P S O N

# JADE AND AMBER'S FLAME SURPRISE

Trout with ginger and garlic on a bed of oriental noodles with a crispy carrot and leek garnish

Margaret Roberts, a registrar of births from Harlow, Essex, told Fern that Jade, Amber and Scarlett – 'a nice set of traffic lights' – were popular new names. Meanwhile Antony cooked up a colourful and delicious dish – and nearly set the studio on fire.

**SERVES 2**

2 x 175–225 g (6–8 oz) trout, gutted and trimmed
6 thin slices of fresh root ginger
2 garlic cloves, finely chopped
1 tablespoon plain flour
$\frac{1}{2}$–1 teaspoon chilli powder, to taste
3 tablespoons olive oil

**FOR THE NOODLES**
4 spring onions
1 vegetable stock cube
3 thin slices of fresh root ginger and
1 teaspoon finely grated ginger

175 g (6 oz) Chinese egg noodles
1 tablespoon vegetable oil
1 garlic clove, finely chopped
1 teaspoon chilli powder
2 tablespoons soy sauce
2 tablespoons dry white wine (optional)
1–2 tablespoons chopped fresh coriander

**FOR THE GARNISH**
Sunflower oil for deep-frying
2 carrots, cut into fine matchsticks
1 leek, cut into fine matchsticks
A few sprigs of coriander

Score the trout on both sides with a sharp knife, then put the ginger slices and garlic in the body cavities. Mix the flour and chilli powder together and sprinkle over the fish. Heat the olive oil in a large frying pan and fry the trout for 5 minutes on each side or until just cooked through. Remove from the heat and keep warm.

While the trout are cooking, prepare the noodles. Finely chop the white parts of the spring onions and set aside; reserve the green tops.

Crumble the stock cube into a pan of water and add the green spring onion tops and the ginger slices. Bring to the boil, then add the noodles and cook for 3 minutes or until just tender. Drain thoroughly and remove the spring onions and ginger slices. Heat the vegetable oil in a pan, add the garlic, grated ginger, chilli and chopped spring onions and cook for 1 minute. Stir in the noodles, soy sauce and wine, if using, and toss until heated through. Stir in the coriander and keep warm.

For the garnish, heat the sunflower oil in a saucepan or deep-fat fryer and deep-fry first the carrots and then the leeks for 2–3 minutes, until they are brown and crispy. Drain on kitchen paper.

To serve, arrange the noodles on 2 warmed serving plates and place the trout on top. Put the carrots and leeks in 2 neat piles on top of the fish and garnish with the sprigs of coriander.

---

### READY STEADY COOK Tip
*The easiest way to cut the carrots into fine matchsticks, or julienne, is to slice them into ribbons with a vegetable peeler, stack up the ribbons, then cut them in half across the centre and slice lengthwise into very fine strips.*

---

# POULTRY AND GAME

BRIAN TURNER

# CHICKEN PRINCIPALITY

Stuffed chicken breasts with mixed vegetables and mead sauce

Sue Hindle from Falmouth enjoys entertaining. She gave Brian some Cornish mead and he showed her how to make a fabulous dish for her next dinner party.

**SERVES 2**

2 eggs, hard-boiled
2 tablespoons finely chopped black olives
15 g (½ oz) butter
3 tomatoes, cut in half
2 baby cauliflowers
100 g (4 oz) green beans
Salt and freshly ground black pepper

**FOR THE CHICKEN**

2 boneless skinless chicken breasts
65 g (2½ oz) butter

1 tablespoon chopped fresh parsley
1 tablespoon plain flour
1 egg, lightly beaten
½ tablespoon double cream
1 tablespoon olive oil

**FOR THE SAUCE**

120 ml (4 fl oz) Cornish mead or red wine
300 ml (10 fl oz) chicken stock
3 sprigs of rosemary
1 tablespoon balsamic vinegar

Pre-heat the oven to gas mark 6, 200°C (400°F).

Slit each chicken breast lengthwise down the centre, being careful not to cut all the way through. Use the knife to fold back the flesh and form a pocket, then flatten slightly with the palms of your hands. Season generously with salt and pepper, then put 25 g (1 oz) of the butter and ½ tablespoon of chopped parsley on each breast. Roll up and coat in the flour. Lightly whisk together the egg and cream and dip the chicken breasts in this mixture. Heat the olive oil and remaining butter in a frying pan, add the chicken and fry for 3 minutes on each side. Transfer to the oven for about 5 minutes to complete the cooking.

Remove the yolks from the hard-boiled eggs and discard (or save to

32

use in sandwiches or salads). Push the egg whites through a sieve and mix with the chopped olives. Melt the butter in a pan, then remove from the heat and stir in the olive mixture.

Season the tomato halves and heat through under a hot grill, cut-side up. Cook the baby cauliflowers and green beans in boiling salted water for about 4 minutes, until just tender, then drain. Keep warm.

To make the sauce, put the mead or red wine, stock and rosemary in a pan and boil until reduced by half. Stir in the balsamic vinegar and simmer for 3 minutes, until the sauce has thickened slightly.

To serve, place each chicken breast in the centre of a warmed serving plate and put the cauliflowers and beans to the side. Place the tomatoes around the edge and pour the sauce over the chicken. Spoon the egg and olive mixture over the chicken and vegetables.

A N T O N Y   W O R R A L L   T H O M P S O N

# THE CHATTANOOGA CHOO CHOO

Spicy chicken with saffron rice, seafood and stuffed tomatoes

Michelle Atkinson's paella was always a disaster. Antony adapted the traditional Spanish dish and named it after her home next to a railway line in Northallerton, Yorkshire.

| | |
|---|---|
| **SERVES 2** | 2 tablespoons olive oil |
| 450 g (1 lb) mussels | 4 tomatoes |
| 175 g (6 oz) basmati rice | 100 g (4 oz) frozen peas |
| 2 good pinches of saffron | 1 onion, finely chopped |
| 75 g (3 oz) butter | 200 ml (7 fl oz) double cream |
| 1 teaspoon dried thyme | 8 large cooked tiger prawns, heads |
| 150 ml (5 fl oz) dry white wine | removed but tails left on |
| 2 chicken drumsticks | 1 tablespoon pitted black olives, halved |
| 1/2 teaspoon cayenne pepper | Salt and freshly ground black pepper |

Pre-heat the oven to gas mark 6, 200°C (400°F).

Clean the mussels by scrubbing them thoroughly under cold running water and removing the beards.

Cook the rice in boiling salted water with 1 pinch of saffron for 10–12 minutes, until just tender, then drain.

Heat 25 g (1 oz) of the butter in a large pan with the thyme and white wine. Add the mussels, cover and cook over a fairly high heat for 2–3 minutes, until the shells have opened, shaking the pan occasionally. Drain, reserving the juices, and discard any mussels that remain closed.

Season the chicken drumsticks with the cayenne. Heat the olive oil in a frying pan and brown the chicken for 5 minutes on each side. Transfer to the oven and roast for 15–20 minutes, until cooked through.

Skin and quarter 2 of the tomatoes and set aside. Cut the other 2 in half and scoop out the seeds.

Cook the peas in boiling salted water for about 3 minutes, then drain. Fry the onion in the remaining butter until soft, then add the peas. Stir in 1 tablespoon of the reserved mussel juices. Fill the tomato halves with a little of this mixture and heat through under a hot grill or in the oven. Add the rice to the remaining onion and peas, season with salt and pepper and stir the mixture thoroughly.

Pour the remaining mussel juice into a separate pan, add the remaining saffron and boil until the liquid is reduced to half its original volume. Stir in the cream and cook gently for about 5 minutes. Season to taste.

To serve, spoon the rice on to 2 warmed serving plates. Place the chicken and stuffed tomatoes in the centre and pour the sauce over the top. Garnish with the mussels, reserved tomato quarters, tiger prawns and olives.

---

### READY STEADY COOK Tip
*When you are cleaning the mussels, if any of them have open shells, tap them firmly with your fingers. The shell should close at once; if not, it means the mussel is dead and should be thrown away.*

## BRIAN TURNER

# POULET SAUTÉ À LA MARMELADE DE JAN

### Fried chicken with marmalade sauce

Jan Perry from Telford, Shropshire, brought a whole chicken and some home-made marmalade
– plus a bottle of tranquillizers in case Brian got into a pickle. Brian kept his cool and cooked
a sumptuous meal.

| SERVES 3–4 | FOR THE SAUCE |
|---|---|
| 350 g (12 oz) small courgettes, grated | 2 tablespoons orange marmalade |
| 3 tablespoons olive oil | 4 tablespoons dry white wine |
| 75 g (3 oz) butter | 300 ml (10 fl oz) chicken stock |
| 1 x 1.25 kg (2 lb 12 oz) chicken, cut into 8 pieces | 50 g (2 oz) butter |
| 1 red and 1 yellow pepper | 1 tablespoon chopped fresh parsley |
| 1 onion, grated | 1 tablespoon chopped fresh dill |
| Salt and freshly ground black pepper | |

Place the grated courgettes in a sieve, sprinkle with salt and leave to
drain while you cook the chicken. Heat 2 tablespoons of the oil and
50 g (2 oz) of the butter in a large shallow pan. Season the chicken
pieces, then add to the pan, skin-side down, and brown on all sides.
Cover and cook for 20–25 minutes, until tender. Remove the chicken
and keep warm. Reserve the juices in the pan.

Cut the red and yellow peppers in half and remove the seeds.
Finely chop half the red and half the yellow pepper and set aside.
Cut each remaining pepper half into 3 strips. Heat the remaining oil
in a ridged grill pan or a frying pan and fry the pepper strips for
about 3 minutes on each side. Sprinkle with salt and set aside.

Rinse and drain the courgettes, pat dry. Heat the remaining butter in a pan and fry the diced pepper for 3 minutes. Add the courgettes and onion, season and cook for a further 3 minutes, until softened.

For the sauce, gently warm the marmalade, then sieve it to remove the peel. Pour the wine into the pan in which the chicken was cooked and bring to the boil, stirring well to scrape up the sediment from the base of the pan. Add the stock, marmalade, butter, parsley and dill and boil rapidly for 3–4 minutes, until reduced to about half its original volume. Taste and adjust the seasoning if necessary.

To serve, spoon the courgette and pepper mixture on to 2 warmed serving plates, lay the pepper strips on top, then arrange the chicken pieces on top of them. Pour the sauce all over.

BRIAN TURNER

# SPINACH-STUFFED CHICKEN LEG ON TURMERIC-BRAISED POTATOES WITH CUMIN-FRIED ONIONS

Yvonne McSherry from Chester can't resist buying spices – even though she never knows what to do with them. She brought along a selection and Brian cooked up a spicy chicken dinner.

**SERVES 2**

2 large chicken legs
3 tablespoons sunflower oil
150 ml (5 fl oz) chicken stock
2 potatoes, diced
150 ml (5 fl oz) dry white wine
5 cardamom pods
50 g (2 oz) butter
1–2 teaspoons turmeric, to taste
1 tablespoon chopped fresh coriander

1 large onion, finely chopped
1 teaspoon ground cumin
Salt and freshly ground black pepper

**FOR THE STUFFING**

100 g (4 oz) fresh spinach
1 egg yolk
3 tablespoons double cream
$1/2$ teaspoon grated fresh root ginger
40 g ($1^1/2$ oz) ground almonds

36

Pre-heat the oven to gas mark 6, 200°C (400°F).

First make the stuffing. Wash the spinach well and put it in a pan with just the water clinging to the leaves. Cook for 3–4 minutes, until wilted, then drain very thoroughly, squeezing out the excess liquid, and chop. Whisk together the egg yolk and cream, then add the spinach, ginger and ground almonds and mix well. Season with salt and pepper.

Remove the thigh bone from each chicken leg by scraping the meat down the bone and pulling it out, leaving a pocket.

Heat 2 tablespoons of the oil in a frying pan and fry the chicken legs, skin-side down, until they begin to brown. Remove from the heat and spoon the spinach stuffing into the pocket in each chicken leg, pressing it in firmly. Fold the chicken flesh up over the stuffing and secure with wooden cocktail sticks. Place each chicken leg on a square of buttered aluminium foil and pour 1 tablespoon of the stock over each one. Wrap securely in the foil, place on a baking sheet and bake in the oven for 15–20 minutes, until the chicken is cooked through.

Heat the remaining oil in a frying pan, add the diced potatoes and fry for 2 minutes. Add the wine and the remaining stock, bring to the boil, then add the cardamom pods and simmer for 5–10 minutes, or until the liquid has reduced by half and the potatoes are tender. Dice half the butter and whisk it into the potatoes with the turmeric. Stir in the coriander, then taste and adjust the seasoning if necessary.

Heat the remaining butter in a separate pan, add the onion and fry until softened but not coloured. Add the cumin and continue to cook until the onion begins to turn brown. Drain off any liquid.

To serve, arrange the onion on 2 warmed serving plates and place the chicken legs on top, removing the cocktail sticks. Surround with the potatoes and their sauce.

---

### READY STEADY COOK Tip
*After boning the chicken legs, flatten them slightly with a cleaver, mallet or rolling pin to make the pocket larger.*

---

B R I A N   T U R N E R

# ATLANTA CHICKEN WITH KUMQUAT CHUTNEY AND ASPARAGUS

*See photograph*

It was love at first sight for American-born Kristen Morrison when policeman Paul came to her rescue. Brian helped her concoct this Valentine's Day dish for him, while he was putting together a sumptuous dessert with Antony (see page 89).

| | |
|---|---|
| **SERVES 2** | 2 tablespoons double cream |
| 1 poussin | 1 tablespoon chopped fresh basil |
| 1 tablespoon olive oil | Salt and freshly ground black pepper |
| 25 g (1 oz) butter | |
| 4 teaspoons Dijon mustard | **FOR THE CHUTNEY** |
| 40 g (1½ oz) cashew nuts, finely ground | 2 shallots, chopped |
| 100 g (4 oz) mixed long grain and wild rice | 1 tablespoon white wine vinegar |
| 10 asparagus spears | 1 tablespoon soft brown sugar |
| 175 ml (6 fl oz) dry white wine | 8 kumquats, quartered |
| 150 ml (5 fl oz) chicken stock | |

Pre-heat the oven to gas mark 6, 200°C (400°F).

To make the chutney, place all the ingredients in a pan, partially cover with a lid and cook over a medium heat for 25–30 minutes.

To prepare the poussin, cut along each side of the backbone with a sharp knife and then remove it. Open the bird out and cut the wishbone in half, or take it out. Put the bird skin-side up on a work surface and press down sharply on the breast with the palm of your hand to flatten it. Cut the poussin in half.

Heat the oil and half the butter in a large frying pan and brown the poussin for 3 minutes on each side. Place in an ovenproof dish, skin-side up, and roast for 20–30 minutes. Half-way through the cooking time, brush the poussin with the mustard and sprinkle the ground cashew nuts on top. Check that the poussin is cooked by inserting a skewer in a leg, near the bone; if the juices run clear it is done.

Cook the rice in boiling salted water until just tender – about 20 minutes or according to the instructions on the packet. Drain and sauté in the remaining butter for 2–3 minutes.

Cut the bottom third off each asparagus spear, slice finely and set aside. Place the asparagus tips in a lightly greased ovenproof dish, pour 2 tablespoons of the white wine over them, cover and bake in the oven for 8–10 minutes. Drain the asparagus if necessary, reserving any liquid.

For the sauce, heat the chicken stock in a pan, add the remaining wine, then boil until reduced to half its original volume. Add the chopped asparagus stalks and any reserved asparagus cooking liquid and continue to cook until the asparagus is tender. Stir in the cream and heat through, then stir in the basil. Season to taste with salt and pepper.

To serve, spoon the rice into the centre of 2 warmed serving plates and put the poussin on top. Spoon the kumquat chutney around the rice and arrange the asparagus tips on top of the chutney. Surround with the sauce.

---

### READY STEADY COOK Tips

• If the chutney becomes too dry while it is cooking, add a little water or white wine to the pan.

• Wild rice is not actually a rice at all but an aquatic grass, grown in North America. Its long black grains are delicious but expensive, and a good way to stretch it is to serve it with long grain white rice. Packets of mixed wild and white rice are now readily available – cook according to packet instructions.

---

## ANTONY WORRALL THOMPSON

# BERTIE'S BUDGET VIRGIN CHICKEN WITH A LITTLE SUMMER SOUP

Chicken breasts and tomatoes stuffed with ricotta and pesto, served with sauce vierge – and perhaps a cucumber and yogurt soup to start

Marilyn Mayes from Hertfordshire asked Antony to cook chicken, her favourite ingredient, and pesto, which she'd never tried before. Antony named this summery dish after Marilyn's pet cockatiel, Bert, who's renowned for mimicking TV theme tunes and has almost mastered the *Ready Steady Cook* theme!

**SERVES 2**
4 small, firm, flavoursome tomatoes
2 boneless skinless chicken breasts
2 tablespoons olive oil
Salt and freshly ground black pepper

1 teaspoon chopped fresh sage
1 tablespoon chopped fresh
mixed parsley and basil
2 teaspoons pesto
$1/2$ small onion, finely chopped

**FOR THE SOUP (OPTIONAL)**
1 cucumber
1 tablespoon chopped onion
or spring onions
200 ml (7 fl oz) Greek yoghurt
1 tablespoon finely chopped fresh mint

**FOR THE SAUCE VIERGE**
$2^1/2$ tablespoons olive oil
1 tablespoon pesto
juice of $1/2$ lemon
3 small, flavoursome tomatoes,
de-seeded and diced
1 tablespoon chopped fresh basil
1 tablespoon chopped fresh parsley

**FOR THE STUFFING**
100 g (4 oz) ricotta cheese
1 egg yolk

If you are making the soup, extract the juice from the cucumber and onion using a centrifugal juice extractor. Whisk in the Greek yoghurt, season to taste with salt and pepper and stir in the chopped mint. Chill thoroughly before serving.

For the chicken, mix together all the ingredients for the stuffing.

Pre-heat the oven to gas mark 6, 200°C (400°F).

Cut the tomatoes in half, scoop out the seeds and leave the tomato halves upside-down on a piece of kitchen paper for a few minutes to drain. Using a sharp knife, slit each chicken breast lengthwise down the centre, being careful not to cut all the way through. Use the knife to fold back the flesh and form a pocket. Stuff the chicken and the tomato halves with the ricotta mixture. Heat the oil in a frying pan, add the chicken and fry for about 5 minutes per side, until cooked through. Put the tomato halves in the oven for 5 minutes to heat through, then place under a hot grill until slightly browned.

To make the sauce, gently heat the oil in a pan, stir in the pesto and heat through, then add the lemon juice and simmer for 1–2 minutes. Add the tomatoes, basil and parsley and cook gently for 2–3 minutes longer.

To serve, arrange the chicken and tomatoes on 2 warmed serving plates and pour over the sauce.

---

### READY STEADY COOK Tips
- *If you don't have a juice extractor for the soup you could process the cucumber and onion in a blender or liquidizer, then press it through a sieve.*
- *If you have time, chill the ricotta mixture for 1–2 hours to firm up before stuffing the chicken and tomatoes.*
- *Sauce vierge is also good with grilled fish.*

---

## BRIAN TURNER

# DANISH-STYLE PHEASANT WITH YORKSHIRE BUBBLE AND SQUEAK

Louisa Greenbaum lives in East London but her favourite foods are influenced by her Danish mother and by Yorkshire, where she grew up. Brian devised a fantastic pheasant dish in honour of both.

**SERVES 2**
2 pheasant breasts
1 tablespoon double cream
2 teaspoons dry white wine
1 teaspoon mustard
Salt and freshly ground black pepper
Sprigs of parsley and dill, to garnish

**FOR THE STUFFING**
2 tablespoons sunflower oil
100 g (4 oz) vacuum-packed chestnuts, roughly chopped
$\frac{1}{2}$ x 275 g (10 oz) tin of blackcurrants
1 tablespoon redcurrant jelly

**FOR THE BUBBLE AND SQUEAK**
350 g (12 oz) potatoes, diced
75 g (3 oz) Brussels sprouts, cut in half
2 tablespoons sunflower oil

**FOR THE BRANDY SAUCE**
1 tablespoon sunflower oil
1 small onion, finely chopped
300 ml (10 fl oz) chicken stock
2 tablespoons brandy
150 ml (5 fl oz) double cream
1 tablespoon finely chopped fresh parsley
1 tablespoon finely chopped fresh dill

Pre-heat the oven to gas mark 6, 200°C (400°F).

First make the stuffing. Heat the oil in a pan, add the chestnuts, drained blackcurrants and redcurrant jelly and simmer for 2–3 minutes, until the mixture is pasty in consistency. Leave to cool.

Put the pheasant breasts in a well-buttered ovenproof dish and season well. Mix together the cream, wine and mustard and spread over the pheasant breasts. Roast in the oven for 8 minutes, basting occasionally. Remove from the oven, cut a pocket in each pheasant breast and fill with the stuffing (any extra can be piled on top). Return to the oven for a further 5 minutes, until cooked through.

To make the bubble and squeak, cook the potatoes in boiling salted water until tender, adding the Brussels sprouts half-way through. Drain and mash together, then season well. Heat the oil in a frying pan and fry the potato mixture until nicely browned, tossing half-way through.

To make the sauce, heat the oil in a frying pan, add the onion and cook gently until softened. Add the stock, brandy, cream, parsley and dill and cook until reduced to about a third of its original volume. Season to taste.

To serve, place the pheasant breasts on a bed of bubble and squeak, pour the sauce over and garnish with parsley and dill sprigs.

### ANTONY WORRALL THOMPSON

# MITCH'S BI-FOCAL CHICKEN

Chicken cooked two ways with carrot rösti, sautéed vegetables and tarragon cream sauce

**Rawle Beckles from London brought along a selection of his favourite ingredients. Antony cooked up a delicious chicken dish in honour of Rawle's wife Mitch.**

**SERVES 2**

300 ml (10 fl oz) chicken stock
85 ml (3 fl oz) dry white wine
2 carrots, sliced
6 shallots, peeled
1 bay leaf
A small handful of fresh tarragon
2 boneless chicken breasts
1 tablespoon olive oil
25 g (1 oz) butter

100 g (4 oz) baby sweetcorn
250 ml (8 fl oz) double cream
A squeeze of lemon juice
Salt and freshly ground black pepper
Flatleaf parsley, to garnish (optional)

**FOR THE CARROT RÖSTI**
3 carrots, grated
1 tablespoon plain flour
1 tablespoon olive oil

Put the stock and white wine in a small pan and add the sliced carrots, whole shallots, bay leaf and the stalks from the tarragon. Bring to a gentle simmer, then add one chicken breast and poach for about 15 minutes, until cooked through. Leave covered in the pan.

Season the remaining chicken breast with salt and pepper. Heat the olive oil and half the butter in a small frying pan, add the chicken skin-side down and brown over a medium heat. Reduce the heat slightly and cook for about 10–15 minutes, turning half-way through.

Cook the baby sweetcorn in boiling water for 2–3 minutes, then drain, refresh in cold water and cut in half lengthways.

To make the carrot rösti, put the grated carrots and flour in a bowl, season well and mix thoroughly. Shape into 2 rounds. Heat the olive oil in a large heavy-based frying pan and carefully transfer the rösti to it, using a fish slice. Fry over a medium-high heat for about 4 minutes on each side, until brown and crisp. (If the rösti start to fall apart when you try to turn them over, cook for a little longer until really crisp underneath.) Drain on kitchen paper.

To make the sauce, pour the cream into a pan and simmer until reduced to about half its original volume. Add 4 tablespoons of the stock in which the chicken was poached and simmer for a further 3–4 minutes, stirring occasionally. Roughly chop the tarragon leaves and stir them into the sauce. Add the lemon juice and season to taste.

Heat the remaining butter in a frying pan and add the baby sweetcorn and the shallots and carrot slices from poaching the chicken. Fry over a medium heat for about 2 minutes, until golden.

To serve, slice both chicken breasts (removing the skin from the poached chicken if preferred). Place the carrot rösti on 2 warmed serving plates and arrange the sliced chicken on top. Surround with the vegetables and pour the tarragon sauce over the poached chicken and around the vegetables. Garnish with flatleaf parsley, if liked.

---

**READY STEADY COOK Tip**
*Shallots are much easier to peel if you pour boiling water over them and leave for about 30 seconds.*

---

## BRIAN TURNER

# POULET FARCI LOUISE BLANDFORD

Chicken on a potato galette with green beans and
lemon butter herb sauce
*See photograph*

Louise Hawkins from Dorset loves cooking and entertaining. She hoped Brian
would help her create a wonderful dish that would persuade Steve,
her partner of 14 years, to marry her.

**SERVES 2**

15 g ($^1/_2$ oz) butter
2 streaky bacon rashers, finely chopped
6 button mushrooms, very finely chopped
2 boneless skinless chicken breasts
1 tablespoon plain flour, seasoned with salt and pepper
1 egg, beaten
2 tablespoons olive oil
100 g (4 oz) green beans
Salt and freshly ground black pepper

**FOR THE POTATO GALETTES**

2 large potatoes, grated
$^1/_2$ onion, grated
1 tablespoon olive oil

**FOR THE SAUCE**

3 tablespoons dry white wine
Juice of $^1/_2$ lemon
150 ml (5 fl oz) double cream
50 g (2 oz) chilled butter, diced
2 tablespoons chopped mixed fresh herbs such
as parsley, basil and tarragon

Melt half the butter in a pan and fry the bacon and mushrooms for
3–4 minutes, until golden. Season with salt and pepper and leave to
cool. With a sharp knife, cut a lengthwise slit down the side of each
chicken breast to form a pocket, being careful not to cut right through.
Stuff with the bacon and mushroom mixture. Coat the chicken with the
seasoned flour then dip in the beaten egg. Fry in the olive oil for
about 5 minutes on each side, until well browned and cooked through.

Meanwhile, make the potato galettes. Put the grated potatoes and onion in a bowl with some salt and pepper and mix well. Heat the olive oil in a large heavy-based frying pan and spoon in the potato and onion mixture in 2 portions, flattening them with the back of the spoon. Fry for about 5 minutes on each side, until golden brown.

Cook the green beans in boiling salted water for 3–4 minutes until just tender. Drain and set aside.

To make the sauce, put the wine and lemon juice in a pan and cook until reduced to about half the original volume. Stir in the cream and heat through. Add the butter a few pieces at a time, whisking constantly, until you have a smooth sauce. Stir in the herbs and season to taste.

To serve, melt the remaining butter in a frying pan, add the green beans and toss for 1–2 minutes just to heat through. Place the potato galettes on 2 warmed serving plates and put the chicken on top. Arrange the green beans to one side and pour the sauce all round.

---

**READY STEADY COOK Tip**
*You could include flavourings in the potato galettes, such as chopped fresh herbs, a pinch of chilli powder, caraway or cumin seeds.*

---

## ANTONY WORRALL THOMPSON

# J.J.'S MAURITIAN FANCY

Deep-fried chicken, okra, banana and sweet potatoes with chicken and pineapple fricassée

Joan Jones, nicknamed J.J., lived in Mauritius for two years, where she had been fascinated by the unusual vegetables in the local market but never dared try them. Now she's returned to Preston, she challenged Antony to recapture the Mauritian sunshine.

**SERVES 2–3**

100 g (4 oz) sweet potato, cut into 1 cm (1/2 inch) dice

Sunflower oil for deep-frying

1 boneless skinless chicken breast, cut into strips

50 g (2 oz) okra, cut lengthwise in half

1 firm banana, cut into 4 cm (1 1/2 inch) chunks

2 tablespoons plain flour

**FOR THE FRICASSÉE**

100 g (4 oz) sweet potato, cut into 1 cm (1/2 inch) dice

2 tablespoons sunflower oil

1 onion, chopped

1/2 teaspoon garam masala

1/2 teaspoon chilli powder

1/2 teaspoon ground cumin

1/2 red pepper, diced

1/2 green pepper, diced

1/2 yellow pepper, diced

1 boneless skinless chicken breast, cut into strips

175 g (6 oz) fresh pineapple, diced

50 g (2 oz) okra, cut into 1 cm (1/2 inch) rounds

2–3 tablespoons crème fraîche

**FOR THE BATTER**

75 g (3 oz) plain flour

A pinch of salt

1 egg

3–4 tablespoons milk

**TO GARNISH**

A few lettuce leaves

A few lemon slices

2 tomatoes, cut into wedges

Cook all the sweet potato, including the potato for the fricassée, in boiling water for 2–3 minutes, then drain and set aside.

For the fricassée, heat the oil in a pan, add the onion and cook gently for 2 minutes. Add the spices and peppers and cook for 2 minutes, then add the chicken, pineapple, okra and 100 g (4 oz) of the par-boiled sweet potato. Simmer gently for 10–15 minutes, until everything is tender, then stir in the crème fraîche and heat through gently.

For the batter, put the flour and salt in a bowl and whisk in the egg, then gradually whisk in enough milk to give the consistency of double cream.

Heat the oil for deep-frying in a saucepan or deep-fat fryer. Coat the chicken pieces, okra, banana and par-boiled sweet potato in the flour and shake off any excess. Dip the chicken in the batter and deep-fry for about 7 minutes, until golden brown and cooked through. Drain on kitchen paper and keep warm. Dip the okra, banana and sweet potato in the remaining batter and deep-fry for about 3 minutes, until golden brown. Drain on kitchen paper.

To serve, arrange the lettuce leaves, lemon slices and tomato wedges around the edge of a serving platter and pile the fried chicken and vegetables in the centre. Serve with the chicken and pineapple fricassée, accompanied by rice or bread.

---

### READY STEADY COOK Tips
• *To check whether the oil is hot enough for deep frying, put in a small cube of bread. If it turns golden brown in about 20 seconds the oil is the correct temperature.*
• *The chicken and pineapple fricassée makes a meal in itself if you serve it with some rice.*

---

## BRIAN TURNER

# HONEY AND LIME CHICKEN WITH ROASTED CELERIAC, CHICKEN LIVER MOUSSE AND MUSHROOM SAUCE

Maureen Travis from Colchester is mother to a very special bouquet – daughters Daisy, Lily, Fleur and Poppy. Brian showed her an ingenious way of serving chicken and chicken livers to make a delicious dish for the whole family.

**SERVES 2**

2 boneless skinless chicken breasts
3 tablespoons runny honey
Juice of $1/2$ lime
Rind of 2 limes
350 g (12 oz) celeriac
2 tablespoons sunflower oil
3 bacon rashers, cut into thin strips
Salt and freshly ground black pepper

**FOR THE MOUSSE**

100 g (4 oz) chicken livers
$1^1/_2$ tablespoons double cream
1 size-1 egg

**FOR THE MUSHROOM SAUCE**

300 ml (10 fl oz) vegetable stock
1 tablespoon dry white wine
4 tablespoons double cream
5 mushrooms, very thinly sliced
25 g (1 oz) butter
1 tablespoon chopped fresh dill

Pre-heat the oven to gas mark 6, 200°C (400°F).

First make the chicken liver mousse. Blend the chicken livers in a food processor until smooth. Add the cream and egg and continue to blend until thoroughly combined. Season with salt and pepper and pour into 2 lightly greased small dariole moulds or ramekin dishes.

Place in a roasting tin, pour enough boiling water into the tin to come two-thirds of the way up the sides of the moulds and bake for about 25 minutes, until the mousse is set.

Coat the chicken with the honey and place in a shallow heatproof dish. Pour over the lime juice and sprinkle with the rind. Leave to marinate for about 10 minutes, if you have time, then cook under a hot grill for 15 minutes, basting regularly and turning half-way through.

Peel the celeriac and scoop it into balls using a melon baller, or cut it into small cubes. Toss it in half the oil, season and then place in a baking tin and roast in the oven for 15–20 minutes. Heat the remaining oil in a pan and fry the bacon until crisp. Add the roasted celeriac and cook for a further 5 minutes, until well browned.

For the mushroom sauce, pour the vegetable stock into a pan and boil over a high heat until reduced to half its original volume. Stir in the white wine, cream, mushrooms, butter and dill and cook gently for 1–2 minutes. Season to taste.

To serve, put the chicken on 2 warmed serving plates and arrange the celeriac and bacon next to it. Run a knife around the edge of each mousse to loosen it, turn it out and place on top of the celeriac mixture, then spoon the mushroom sauce over the mousse.

---

### READY STEADY COOK Tips

• *Most chicken livers come ready trimmed these days but, if necessary, cut off any tubes or membranes and green patches before use. Any leftover livers will freeze well.*
• *If your food processor is too large to purée such small quantities for the chicken liver mousse, use a liquidizer or a hand blender.*
• *If you have time to prepare it in advance, leave the chicken to marinate for several hours, covered, in the refrigerator.*

---

## BRIAN TURNER

# STUFFED TURKEY STEAKS WITH BEAN STEW AND DINO PASTA

Janet Brook now lives in Cornwall but originally came from Yorkshire, and was keen to cook with a fellow Yorkshireman. As the ultimate challenge, Janet's grandson had insisted she bring along dinosaur-shaped pasta, saying, 'Brian will know what to do with it.'

**SERVES 2**

2 x 175 g (6 oz) thick turkey breast steaks
1 tablespoon olive oil
25 g (1 oz) butter
Juice of 1/2 lemon
Salt and freshly ground black pepper

**FOR THE PASTA**

50 g (2 oz) dinosaur pasta or other pasta shapes
1 tablespoon olive oil
3 plum tomatoes, quartered
15 g (1/2 oz) butter

**FOR THE BEAN STEW**

4 tablespoons olive oil
1 small aubergine, finely diced
1 garlic clove, crushed
3 slices of ham, finely diced
1 x 425 g (15 oz) tin of haricot beans, drained
2 tablespoons double cream
2 tablespoons chopped fresh basil

**FOR THE FRIED ONIONS**

Sunflower oil for deep-frying
1 onion, sliced
2 tablespoons milk
25–50 g (1–2 oz) plain flour, seasoned with salt and pepper

Cook the pasta in boiling salted water for about 8 minutes or until *al dente*, then drain and set aside.

Carefully cut a lengthwise slit in each turkey steak to form a pocket (like pitta bread). Drizzle the olive oil over them and cook on a ridged grill pan or in a heavy-based frying pan for 6–10 minutes on each side, depending on their thickness.

To make the bean stew, heat the oil in a pan, add the aubergine and fry for 3 minutes. Add the garlic and ham, season with salt and pepper and cook for 5 minutes longer. Stir in the haricot beans and heat through. Add the cream and simmer for 2–3 minutes, then add the basil. Taste and adjust the seasoning if necessary. Spoon 2 tablespoons of the bean stew into the pocket of each turkey steak and keep warm in a low oven.

For the pasta, heat the olive oil in a frying pan, add the tomatoes and fry for 3 minutes. Stir in the drained pasta and the butter, season to taste and toss well.

For the fried onions, heat the sunflower oil in a saucepan or deep-fat fryer. Dip the onion slices in the milk and then in the seasoned flour and deep-fry until golden brown. Drain on kitchen paper.

Melt the butter in a small pan, then remove from the heat and stir in the lemon juice.

To serve, spoon the bean stew on to 2 warmed serving plates. Pile the pasta mixture on top and arrange the stuffed turkey steaks on top of that. Pour over the lemon butter and garnish with the fried onions.

---

### READY STEADY COOK Tip
*Pork steaks could be substituted for the turkey steaks.*
*If they are very thin, there is no need to stuff them.*

---

# MEAT DISHES

## ANTONY WORRALL THOMPSON

# MATA HARI'S MOTHER'S MEZE

Chick pea salad, couscous salad with spicy sausage, and grilled vegetables with yoghurt dip

Pauline Robinson lives in Marlow, Buckinghamshire, but her husband works in Turkey. She brought along a selection of Mediterranean and Middle Eastern ingredients and Antony cooked up three tasty dishes.

**SERVES 2**

1 courgette, sliced lengthwise
1 small head of radicchio, cut into wedges
1 tablespoon olive oil
A few lettuce leaves
175 g (6 oz) kabanos sausage (spicy cured sausage), sliced
1 tablespoon chopped fresh parsley
1 tablespoon balsamic vinegar
Salt and freshly ground black pepper

**FOR THE COUSCOUS SALAD**

100 g (4 oz) couscous
1 courgette, sliced
A pinch of ground coriander
A pinch of ground turmeric
A pinch of ground cinnamon
40 g (1½ oz) sultanas
3 small tomatoes, finely diced
1 tablespoon olive oil

**FOR THE CHICK PEA SALAD**

1 x 425 g (15 oz) tin of chick peas, drained
A pinch of ground coriander
A pinch of ground turmeric
2 pinches of ground cumin
A pinch of ground cinnamon
2 tablespoons olive oil
¼ small onion, finely chopped
3 small tomatoes, cut into quarters and de-seeded
1 tablespoon chopped fresh basil
1 tablespoon balsamic vinegar
2 tablespoons chopped fresh coriander

**FOR THE YOGHURT DIP**

¼ cucumber, peeled, de-seeded and finely diced
2 teaspoons chopped fresh mint
150 ml (5 fl oz) Greek yoghurt

For the couscous salad, put the couscous in a bowl, pour over hot water to cover and leave for about 10 minutes, until the couscous is tender and the water has been absorbed. Lightly boil or steam the courgette until just tender. Mix together the couscous, spices, courgette, sultanas, tomatoes and olive oil, then season to taste.

For the chick pea salad, mix together all the ingredients except 1 tablespoon of the fresh coriander and season with salt and pepper.

For the yoghurt dip, mix together all the ingredients and season with salt and pepper.

Brush the courgette slices and radicchio wedges with the olive oil and cook under a hot grill for about 1 minute per side, until the courgette is golden brown and the radicchio is slightly softened.

To serve, put the lettuce leaves on a plate and spoon the couscous salad on top. Arrange the sausage slices on top of the salad and sprinkle with the parsley. Put the chick pea salad in a bowl and garnish with the remaining coriander. Arrange the grilled radicchio and courgette on a plate and drizzle over the balsamic vinegar. Serve with the yoghurt dip.

## BRIAN TURNER

# HAM WITH HOT PINEAPPLE CHUTNEY

**Katrina Mudge from Newbury wanted Brian to show her how to cook sweet with savoury, so she brought along some gammon, pineapple and sweet potatoes.**

| | |
|---|---|
| **SERVES 2** | 75 g (3 oz) butter |
| 100 g (4 oz) spring greens, finely shredded, plus 4–6 whole leaves | 1 small onion, sliced |
| 3 tablespoons white wine vinegar | 2 tablespoons honey |
| $^1/_2$ pineapple (about 225 g/8 oz) | 300 g (11 oz) gammon steak, cut into 4 medallions |
| 300 g (11 oz) sweet potatoes | Salt and freshly ground black pepper |

Pre-heat the oven to gas mark 4, 180°C (350°F).

Put the shredded spring greens in a serving dish. Bring the vinegar to the boil in a small pan and pour it over the greens. Leave to soak for about 15 minutes.

Peel the pineapple. Finely dice half the flesh and cut the rest into 2.5 cm (1 inch) rounds with a pastry cutter or cut into wedges. Peel the sweet potatoes and cut them into slices 1 cm ($\frac{1}{2}$ inch thick). Cut these into 2.5 cm (1 inch) rounds or into wedges, like the pineapple. Cook the sweet potatoes in boiling salted water for 5 minutes until just tender, then drain and set aside.

To make the pineapple chutney, melt 25 g (1 oz) of the butter in a small pan, add the finely diced pineapple and cook for 3 minutes. Add the onion and honey and cook gently for about 10 minutes, until the onion is soft. Season to taste with salt and pepper.

Cut the stalks out of the whole spring green leaves, then blanch the leaves in a frying pan of boiling water for 1–2 minutes, until just softened. Drain, then spread flat and pat dry. Place 1 tablespoon of the chutney in the centre of each leaf, then wrap up to form a parcel. Place in a shallow ovenproof dish with 25 g (1 oz) of the butter and bake for about 5 minutes, until the butter has melted.

Heat the remaining butter in a frying pan, add the sweet potatoes and the pineapple circles or wedges and cook until golden brown on both sides.

Cook the gammon on a lightly oiled ridged grill pan or in a heavy frying pan for 4–5 minutes on each side.

To serve, arrange alternate pieces of pineapple and sweet potato in an overlapping circle around the edge of each serving plate. Place the gammon and the chutney parcels in the middle and pour the melted butter from the parcels over the top. The shredded spring greens should be served separately as a salad.

---

### READY STEADY COOK Tip
*Make some extra pineapple chutney and serve it with other meat dishes. It will keep in the fridge for up to a week.*

---

## ANTONY WORRALL THOMPSON

# AINSLIE'S ALTERNATIVE MUNCH BRUNCH WITH A CRUNCH

Baked brioche filled with pork and sage patties, mushrooms, bacon-wrapped tomatoes, fried eggs and fried onion rings

Sue Hansen's husband likes nothing more than a fry-up of his favourite ingredients – sausage, bacon, eggs and mushrooms. Antony created a bumper breakfast dish that's delicious at any time of day.

**SERVES 4**

1 brioche loaf or 8 individual brioches
6 streaky bacon rashers, rinds removed
6 small tomatoes, cut in half
15 g ( $\frac{1}{2}$ oz) butter
100 g (4 oz) button mushrooms
$\frac{1}{2}$ teaspoon chopped fresh sage
A squeeze of lemon juice
4 eggs
1 tablespoon sunflower oil
Salt and freshly ground black pepper

**FOR THE FRIED ONION RINGS**

100 g (4 oz) plain flour, plus extra for dusting
1 egg
150 ml (5 fl oz) milk
Sunflower oil for deep-frying
1 onion, sliced into rings

**FOR THE PATTIES**

450 g (1 lb) sausagemeat
2 teaspoons chopped fresh sage
$\frac{1}{2}$ teaspoon ground coriander
1 tablespoon olive oil

Pre-heat the oven to gas mark 6, 200°C (400°F).

If you are using a brioche loaf, slice it in half lengthwise and, leaving the crust intact, scoop out the centre. If you are using individual brioches, cut off the tops and scoop out the centre. Process the scooped-out brioche in a food processor or liquidizer to make breadcrumbs. Place the 2 brioche halves or the individual brioches in the oven for about 5 minutes, until just beginning to brown.

Next make the batter for the fried onion rings. Whisk together the flour, egg and milk, season with salt and pepper and set aside.

For the patties, mix together the sausagemeat, sage and coriander, season and knead lightly. Shape into 8 small patties and coat with the brioche crumbs (you may not need them all). Fry in the olive oil for about 5 minutes on each side, until browned and cooked through.

Stretch the bacon rashers by running the back of a knife along each one, then cut them in half. Wrap 1 piece of bacon around each tomato half, put on long skewers and place under a hot grill until the bacon is cooked and the tomato halves soft.

Heat the butter in a small pan, add the mushrooms, sage and lemon juice and fry for 3–4 minutes until softened, then season.

For the onion rings, heat the oil for deep-frying in a saucepan or deep-fat fryer. Dust the onion rings with flour, dip them in the batter and deep-fry for 1–2 minutes, until golden brown. Drain well on kitchen paper.

Heat the tablespoon of sunflower oil in a pan and fry the eggs.

To serve, fill the brioche halves with the bacon-wrapped tomatoes, mushrooms and meat patties and put the fried eggs on top (if using small brioches put the tomatoes and mushrooms inside and place the meat patties and fried eggs beside them). Garnish with the onion rings.

---

### READY STEADY COOK Tip
*If you don't have time to make the batter for the onion rings, just dip them in a little milk, then a little seasoned flour, before deep-frying.*

---

## BRIAN TURNER

# BOEUF GRILLÉ, SALADE DE CHAMPIGNONS, SAUCE HOLLANDAISE

Spicy beef steak with warm mushroom salad
and hollandaise sauce

Rachel O'Hara, a colour consultant from Billericay, Essex, brought along
some stylish ingredients and Brian cooked a meal that
looked as good as it tasted.

**SERVES 2**

1 teaspoon ground coriander
1 teaspoon ground cumin
1 teaspoon paprika
1 teaspoon cayenne pepper
2 x 175 g (6 oz) sirloin steaks
4 tablespoons olive oil
6 shallots, peeled
1 tablespoon caster sugar
1 large or 2 medium potatoes,
thinly sliced lengthwise
100 g (4 oz) green beans, cut into
1 cm (¹/₂ inch) lengths
Salt and freshly ground black pepper

**FOR THE MUSHROOM SALAD**

1 tablespoon olive oil
150 g (5 oz) oyster mushrooms, sliced
1 tablespoon white wine vinegar

**FOR THE HOLLANDAISE SAUCE**

1 size-1 egg yolk
2 teaspoons white wine vinegar
100 g (4 oz) butter, melted
1 tablespoon chopped fresh parsley

Pre-heat the oven to gas mark 6, 200°C (400°F).

Mix together the spices and coat the steaks with them. Heat 1
tablespoon of the oil in a heavy-based frying pan and fry the steaks for
3–5 minutes on each side, depending on how you like them done.

Cook the shallots in a pan of boiling water for 3–5 minutes, until softened. Drain and pat dry, then place in a small casserole dish or ovenproof frying pan with 1 tablespoon of the olive oil, sprinkle with the sugar and fry for about 2 minutes. Transfer to the oven and cook for 10 minutes, until golden.

Heat the remaining oil in a frying pan and fry the potato slices until tender and golden brown, adding salt and pepper to taste.
Meanwhile, make the mushroom salad. Heat the oil in a frying pan, add the mushrooms and fry for 2–3 minutes, until tender. Transfer the mushrooms to a small bowl, season with salt and pepper and then stir in the vinegar and 1 tablespoon of water.

Cook the green beans in boiling salted water for 3–4 minutes, until just tender, then drain and season. Keep warm.

To make the hollandaise sauce, whisk the egg yolk, vinegar and $1/2$ tablespoon of water together in a small pan for 3 minutes over a very gentle heat. Slowly add the melted butter, whisking continuously, until the sauce thickens but still has a pouring consistency. Season to taste and stir in the parsley.

To serve, arrange the fried potatoes and shallots on 2 warmed serving plates. Pile the beans in the centre and put the steaks on top. Spoon the mushroom salad around the outside and pour the hollandaise sauce over the steaks.

---

### READY STEADY COOK Tip
*Hollandaise sauce is not as difficult to make as many people think and is very quick. The secret is to add the melted butter in a very thin stream and to keep the heat as low as possible, otherwise the egg will scramble. Keep lifting the pan off the heat as you add the butter, to prevent the mixture getting too hot.*

---

## ANTONY WORRALL THOMPSON

# TOYS AREN'T US

### Pork and new potato pie with red Leicester cheese

Zoë Stewart from Norfolk has two children who refuse to eat anything she cooks for them.
Antony devised an imaginative dish they wouldn't be able to resist.

**SERVES 3–4**
675 g (1½ lb) new potatoes
2 tablespoons olive oil
2 shallots, finely chopped
3 garlic cloves, finely chopped
1 x 400 g (14 oz) tin of chopped tomatoes
1 teaspoon dried thyme or Italian mixed herbs

150 ml (5 fl oz) dry white wine or stock
25 g (1 oz) butter
450 g (1 lb) minced pork
1 tablespoon tomato purée
100 g (4 oz) red Leicester cheese, grated
Salt and freshly ground black pepper

Cut 350 g (12 oz) of the potatoes lengthwise in half and roughly
chop the rest. Cook them separately in boiling salted water until
tender and then drain.

Heat half the oil in a frying pan and fry the shallots and two-thirds of
the garlic for about 5 minutes, until soft. Add the tomatoes, dried
herbs and white wine or stock and simmer for 10–12 minutes.
Season with salt and pepper.

Heat the butter and the remaining oil in a separate pan, add the
minced pork and cook until browned. Add the remaining garlic and
cook for 2–3 minutes, then stir in the tomato purée and tomato sauce
and continue to simmer for about 15 minutes, until the pork is
completely cooked.

Put the chopped potatoes in a shallow ovenproof dish large enough
to hold them in a single layer. Spread the pork mixture on top and
arrange the halved potatoes, cut-side up, on top of that. Cover with
the grated cheese and place in a hot oven or under a hot grill for 5
minutes, until the cheese has melted.

## BRIAN TURNER

# TINA TURNER'S BREAKFAST

Fried kidneys and bacon on carrot purée with mushroom
and coriander sauce

To the embarrassment of her grandchildren, Rita Jones from Abberley, Worcestershire, did an impromptu impression of her favourite singer, Tina Turner. Meanwhile Brian was busy cooking her favourite ingredients – kidneys and bacon.

**SERVES 2**
225 g (8 oz) carrots, sliced
3 tablespoons Greek yoghurt
450 g (1 lb) lamb's kidneys
25 g (1 oz) butter
2 tablespoons olive oil
1 small onion, sliced
2 bacon rashers, thinly sliced
2 tablespoons thinly sliced fresh basil

Salt and freshly ground black pepper

**FOR THE SAUCE**
300 ml (10 fl oz) chicken stock
2 tablespoons damson wine or sweet sherry
25 g (1 oz) butter
6 small open-cap mushrooms, sliced
2 tablespoons chopped fresh coriander

Cook the carrots in boiling salted water until tender, then drain. Add the Greek yoghurt and some salt and pepper, then mash until smooth. Keep warm.

Drain the kidneys over a bowl, slice them in half lengthways and remove the white core and the fat. Heat the butter and half the oil in a pan and fry the kidneys for 4–5 minutes; they should be browned on the outside but still pink in the centre.

Meanwhile, make the sauce. Put the chicken stock and wine or sherry in a pan and boil until reduced to half its original volume. Heat the butter in a separate pan, add the mushrooms and fry for 3–4 minutes, until tender. Drain and add them to the reduced stock with the coriander. Season to taste and keep warm.

Fry the onion in the remaining oil for 3–4 minutes, until softened, then add the bacon, raise the heat and cook for a further 3 minutes to brown the onion and crisp the bacon.

To serve, spread the carrot purée on 2 warmed serving plates and arrange the fried bacon and onion on top. Place the kidneys on top of the bacon mixture and pour the sauce around the edge and over the kidneys. Sprinkle the basil over the top.

ANTONY WORRALL THOMPSON

# JET-LAG STEAK STACK

Antony had stepped off a plane from Australia only hours earlier but was still able to rustle up this stunning meal for Jane Saxon from Thornton Cleveleys, Lancashire.

**SERVES 2**
175 g (6 oz) very thin slices of fillet steak (8–10 slices)
1 x 100 g (4 oz) Mozzarella cheese in water, drained and cut into 8 slices
6 basil leaves, shredded
Salt and freshly ground black pepper

**FOR THE TOMATO SAUCE**
3 tablespoons olive oil
1 onion, finely chopped
2 garlic cloves, finely chopped

1 teaspoon dried thyme
1 x 400 g (14 oz) tin of chopped tomatoes

**FOR THE POTATO PANCAKES**
350 g (12 oz) potatoes, grated
50 g (2 oz) butter, melted
2 tablespoons olive oil

**FOR THE GREEN BEAN SALAD**
100 g (4 oz) green beans
2 tablespoons finely chopped onion
2 tablespoons olive oil
2 teaspoons balsamic vinegar

First make the tomato sauce. Heat the olive oil in a frying pan and fry the onion for 3 minutes, then stir in the garlic and thyme. Add the tomatoes and simmer for 8–10 minutes. Season with salt and pepper.

For the potato pancakes, dry the grated potatoes on kitchen paper, then mix with the melted butter and some salt and pepper. Heat the oil in a large frying pan and spoon in the potato mixture in 2 portions, flattening them with the back of the spoon. Fry for 4–5 minutes on each side, until golden and crisp. Remove from the pan and keep warm.

For the salad, cook the green beans in boiling salted water for about 4 minutes, until just tender, then drain and refresh under cold running water. Mix with the onion, oil and balsamic vinegar. Toss together lightly and season to taste.

Season the steaks and cook them quickly on both sides in the pan in which the potato pancakes were cooked; they should take only 30 seconds to 1 minute, depending on thickness.

Assemble the steak stacks as follows: put each potato cake on a heatproof plate and arrange alternate layers of steak, Mozzarella and a little tomato sauce on top, ending with a large slice of Mozzarella. Place under the grill or in a very hot oven for a few minutes until the cheese melts.

To serve, put the green bean salad beside the steak stacks and pour the remaining tomato sauce on top. Garnish with the basil.

---

## READY STEADY COOK Tips

- *If you prefer a smoother texture, purée the tomato sauce in a liquidizer or food processor.*
- *Balsamic vinegar has a rich, mellow, sour-sweet flavour and, although it isn't cheap, a little goes a long way. Just a few drops will perk up many dishes, such as salads, fish and meat and even fresh strawberries.*

B R I A N   T U R N E R

# THE HUMBER BRIDGE VEGETABLE HOTPOT

Meatballs with couscous, vegetables and
mint and yoghurt sauce
*See photograph*

Mother-of-four Beverley Beedham from South Humberside is used to cooking on a tight
budget. Brian showed her how to turn meatballs and couscous into a North African feast that
doesn't break the bank.

**SERVES 2**
300 ml (10 fl oz) beef stock
150 ml (5 fl oz) dry white wine
100 g (4 oz) couscous
50 g (2 oz) butter
1 courgette, diced
1 large tomato, diced
2 carrots, diced
100 g (4 oz) frozen broad beans
1 x 425 g (15 oz) tin of chick peas, drained
Salt and freshly ground black pepper
Flatleaf parsley, to garnish

**FOR THE SAUCE**
1 tablespoon finely chopped fresh mint
4 tablespoons double cream
juice of $1/2$ lemon
4 tablespoons Greek yoghurt

**FOR THE MEATBALLS**
225 g (8 oz) minced steak
1 tablespoon grated onion
1 egg yolk
1–2 teaspoons Worcestershire sauce, to taste

First make the sauce. Put all the ingredients into a bowl, season with
salt and pepper and stir well to combine. Set aside.

Pour the beef stock and wine into a shallow saucepan or a frying
pan and heat to simmering point. Place the couscous in a bowl and
pour over boiling water to cover. Add a little of the hot stock, then
cover with cling film and leave for 10 minutes, until the couscous is

softened and all the liquid has been absorbed.

For the meatballs, mix together all the ingredients with some salt and pepper. Shape into 2.5 cm (1 inch) balls and poach in the simmering stock for about 5 minutes or until just cooked through (remove one from the pan and test with a knife).

Heat 25 g (1 oz) of the butter in a frying pan, add the courgette and tomato and cook gently for about 5 minutes, until the courgette is just tender. Season to taste and keep warm. Cook the carrots and broad beans separately in boiling salted water until just tender, then drain. Melt half the remaining butter in a pan, add the broad beans and the drained chick peas and toss until the chick peas are heated through. Toss the carrots in the remaining butter.

To serve, arrange the couscous on a heated serving platter, place the meatballs on top and spoon over the yoghurt sauce. Arrange the vegetables in small piles around the edge and garnish with flatleaf parsley.

---

### READY STEADY COOK Tips

• *Couscous stews are traditionally served with harissa, a fiery North African spice paste. Add 1/2 teaspoon, or to taste, to the meatballs or the yoghurt sauce, if liked.*

• *Other vegetables can be substituted for the courgette, carrots and broad beans, such as peppers, fennel, leeks or green beans.*

---

## ANTONY WORRALL THOMPSON

# LYNN'S STEAK OF MANY COLOURS

Steak and ratatouille with polenta and grilled vegetables
*See photograph*

Lynn Manning from Newcastle upon Tyne was keen to cook something colourful to impress her partner, Paul. Polenta, red pepper and aubergine fitted the bill perfectly – and are just the sort of ingredients Antony enjoys cooking with.

| SERVES 2 | |
|---|---|
| 175 g (6 oz) quick-cook polenta | 1 teaspoon dried thyme |
| 450 ml (15 fl oz) water | 1 teaspoon dried oregano |
| 2 courgettes | 4 tablespoons dry white wine |
| 1 large aubergine | 2 tablespoons tomato purée |
| 1 red pepper | 2 x 150 g (5 oz) fillet steaks |
| 2 tablespoons olive oil | 1 tablespoon chopped fresh basil |
| 1/2 onion, finely chopped | 1 teaspoon chopped fresh thyme |
| 4 garlic cloves, finely chopped | Salt and freshly ground black pepper |

Cook the polenta in the water with a pinch of salt according to the instructions on the packet. Spoon it into an oiled 18 x 28 x 2.5 cm (7 x 11 x 1 inch) baking tin and spread out in a layer about 2 cm (3/4 inch) thick. Leave to cool, then use a pastry cutter to cut out 4 circles 10 cm (4 inch) in diameter.

Dice 1 courgette and cut the other on the diagonal into slices 1 cm (1/2 inch) thick. Cut 4 slices from the aubergine, 1 cm (1/2 inch) thick, and dice the rest. Set aside.

Cut the red pepper in half and remove the seeds, then trim each half into a neat square; dice the trimmings. Cook the red pepper squares under a hot grill for 10 minutes, until the skin chars and blisters. Leave until cool enough to handle, then peel off the skin.

For the ratatouille, heat the oil in a pan, add the onion, garlic, red pepper trimmings, dried thyme and oregano and cook gently until the onion is translucent. Add the diced courgette and aubergine and cook for 4 minutes. Stir in the wine and tomato purée, season with salt and pepper, then cover and simmer for 20–30 minutes, adding a little water if the mixture becomes too dry.

Cook the courgette and aubergine slices on a lightly oiled ridged grill pan for about 7 minutes, until browned (or brush them with oil and cook them under the grill). Remove from the pan and keep warm.

Season the steak. Cook the steak and the polenta circles on a ridged grill pan or under a hot grill. The steak will take about 3 minutes on each side (for rare steak); the polenta circles are done when they form a golden crust.

To serve, build 2 stacks by layering a polenta circle, aubergine slice, pepper square, aubergine slice, courgette slices, polenta circle. Place each stack on a serving plate, spoon the ratatouille to one side and arrange the steak on top of the ratatouille. Sprinkle the steak with the basil and fresh thyme.

---

### READY STEADY COOK Tips

• *After grilling the red pepper, put it in a plastic bag for a few minutes and seal. The steam created softens the pepper, making it easier to peel.*

• *To use up the polenta trimmings, cut them into pieces and layer in a casserole dish with a well-flavoured cheese sauce, or with a tomato sauce and sliced cheese such as gorgonzola or Parmesan. Bake in the oven at gas mark 6, 200°C (400°F) until brown and bubbling.*

• *Any leftover ratatouille will keep in the fridge for several days and can be used to fill tarts or omelettes or tossed with pasta.*

## BRIAN TURNER

# PORK SPÄTZLE

Pork in mushroom and soured cream sauce with noodles
and green cabbage

Forever bickering about who was the better cook, mother and daughter Jenny and Ruth
Mortimer from Wilmslow, Cheshire, challenged one another on *Ready Steady Cook*. Brian
cooked Jenny this tasty pork dish with German noodles.

**SERVES 2**
1 tablespoon olive oil
50 g (2 oz) butter
1 small onion, chopped
225–275 g (8–10 oz) pork fillet, cut into
1 cm (½ inch) cubes
100 g (4 oz) button mushrooms, quartered
2 teaspoons paprika

250 ml (8 fl oz) soured cream
Lemon juice, to taste
175 g (6 oz) spätzle (German noodles) or
other dried noodles
175 g (6 oz) green cabbage, finely shredded
1 tablespoon chopped fresh parsley
Salt and freshly ground black pepper

Heat the oil and half the butter in a frying pan, add the onion and
cook gently until soft. Add the pork and cook until it is beginning to
brown, then stir in the mushrooms and cook for 5 minutes. Cover and
cook for 5–10 minutes longer, until the pork is tender. Stir in the
paprika and cook for 1 minute, then season with salt and pepper. Stir
in the soured cream and heat through but do not allow the mixture to
boil. Add lemon juice to taste.

Cook the noodles in boiling salted water until just tender (dried
spätzle will take about 15 minutes; other noodles only 8–10 minutes).
Drain and toss with half the remaining butter and some salt and pepper.

Cook the cabbage in boiling salted water for 2 minutes, then drain.
Return it to the pan and stir in the remaining butter.

To serve, arrange small piles of the noodles and cabbage around
the edges of 2 warmed serving plates. Spoon the pork and mushroom
mixture into the centre and sprinkle over the chopped parsley.

ANTONY WORRALL THOMPSON

# SPAGHETTI BOLOGNESE BLACK WATCH BEETLE
*See photograph*

Kathleen Fiddes' family in Midlothian, Scotland, love pasta but she'd run out of ideas on how to cook it. Antony gave her plenty of inspiration with this recipe and the one on page 72.

| SERVES 4 | |
|---:|---|
| 2 tablespoons olive oil | 1 tablespoon tomato purée |
| 2 onions, chopped | 4 tablespoons red wine |
| 3 garlic cloves, crushed | 1 tablespoon chopped fresh parsley |
| 2 teaspoons mixed dried herbs | 5 drops of Tabasco sauce |
| 675 g (1½ lb) minced beef | 450 g (1 lb) spaghetti |
| 1 beef stock cube | 2 tablespoons chopped fresh basil |
| 1 x 400 g (14 oz) tin of chopped tomatoes | Salt and freshly ground black pepper |
| | Freshly grated Parmesan cheese, to serve |

Heat the oil in a pan, add the onions and cook gently until translucent.

Add the garlic, mixed herbs and minced beef and cook for 5 minutes, until the meat is browned. Crumble in the stock cube and stir in the tomatoes, tomato purée, red wine, parsley and Tabasco. Season and simmer for at least 10 minutes, until the mince is completely cooked. Ideally, if you have time, add a little water and cook slowly for 40 minutes until the sauce has thickened and reduced. Taste and adjust the seasoning, if necessary.

Cook the spaghetti in a large pan of boiling salted water for 8 minutes or until *al dente*, then drain.

To serve, pour the sauce over the spaghetti, sprinkle with the basil and accompany with the Parmesan cheese.

## BRIAN TURNER

# FILLET OF PORK TOUT LE MONDE

Pork with mixed vegetables and mushroom and prune sauce
*See photograph*

Vicky Potter from Uxbridge was lacking in ideas when it came to cooking pork. Brian changed all that when he combined pork and prunes to make a dish her RAF family adored.

**SERVES 2**

3 celery sticks, cut in half
3 tablespoons olive oil
1 onion, cut into rings
1 green pepper, sliced
$1/2$ teaspoon chilli powder
1 small egg
$1^1/_2$ tablespoons double cream
350 g (12 oz) piece of pork fillet, cut in half and fat removed
2 tablespoons plain flour, seasoned with salt and pepper
25 g (1 oz) butter

Salt and freshly ground black pepper
Chopped fresh parsley, to garnish

**FOR THE SAUCE**

75 g (3 oz) chilled butter
100 g (4 oz) button mushrooms, chopped
8 ready-to-eat prunes, chopped
300 ml (10 fl oz) chicken stock
2 tablespoons dry white wine
2 tablespoons double cream
4 tablespoons white wine vinegar
1 teaspoon grainy or Dijon mustard

First make the sauce. Heat 25 g (1 oz) of the butter in a pan, add the mushrooms and fry for 2–3 minutes, until just tender. Add the prunes and fry for 1 minute, then remove the pan from the heat and set aside. Put the stock and white wine into a separate pan and boil until reduced to just under half its original volume. Add the cream and simmer for a few minutes until it is slightly reduced.

In a small pan, boil the vinegar until it is reduced to 1 tablespoon. Add to the sauce with the mustard. Cut up the remaining butter and whisk it into the sauce a few pieces at a time, until smooth. Simmer the sauce again until reduced to about 150 ml (5 fl oz). Stir in the mushrooms and prunes and season to taste with salt and pepper. Keep warm.

Cook the celery in boiling water for 10 minutes, then drain.

Heat 2 tablespoons of the olive oil in a frying pan and fry the onion and green pepper with the chilli powder until softened. Meanwhile, lightly whisk together the egg and cream. Flatten the pork fillet slightly with the palm of your hand, then coat it in the seasoned flour, shaking off any excess. Dip the meat in the egg and cream and then fry in the butter and the remaining oil for about 8–10 minutes, turning the fillets over half-way through.

To serve, arrange the vegetables on 2 warmed serving plates, place the pork on top and pour over the sauce. Garnish with parsley.

A N T O N Y   W O R R A L L   T H O M P S O N

# FARFALLE CARBONARA

*See photograph*

| SERVES 4 | 2 egg yolks |
|---:|:---|
| 450 g (1 lb) dried farfalle pasta | 300 ml (10 fl oz) double cream |
| 1 tablespoon olive oil | 1 tablespoon chopped fresh parsley |
| 6 bacon rashers, finely sliced | 2 tablespoons chopped fresh basil |
| 4 tablespoons dry white wine | Salt and freshly ground black pepper |

Cook the pasta in a large pan of boiling salted water for 8 minutes or until *al dente*, then drain. Meanwhile, make the sauce. Heat the oil in a frying pan, add the bacon and fry for 5–7 minutes, adding the white wine half-way through the cooking time. Beat the egg yolks and cream together, then stir in the parsley and some salt and pepper. Add to the bacon and heat through gently without letting it boil.

To serve, pour the sauce over the drained pasta, mix well and sprinkle the basil over the top.

ANTONY WORRALL THOMPSON

# BLACK PUDDING À LA FORESTIÈRE WITH PIEDMONTESE PEPPERS

*See photograph*

Janet Aitken from Berkshire has two passions, cooking and travel. Her ingredients were a mix of the exotic and the traditional and Antony gave homely black pudding a delicious Mediterranean twist with a dish of baked peppers.

**SERVES 2**
350 g (12 oz) potatoes, diced
75 g (3 oz) butter
1 tablespoon Greek yoghurt
5 small Cox's apples, peeled, cored and diced
Juice of 1 lemon
$^1/_2$ onion, diced
2 bay leaves
1 teaspoon caster sugar
$^1/_4$ teaspoon freshly grated nutmeg
1 teaspoon dried thyme

1 tablespoon olive oil
1 black pudding, sliced on the diagonal
Salt and freshly ground black pepper

**FOR THE PIEDMONTESE PEPPERS**
2 thin slices of onion
2 small tomatoes, cut in half and de-seeded
1 pepper, cut in half and de-seeded
$^1/_2$ teaspoon dried thyme
1 tablespoon olive oil

Pre-heat the oven to gas mark 6, 200°C (400°F).

For the Piedmontese peppers, place 1 onion slice and 2 tomato halves in each pepper half, sprinkle with the thyme and then drizzle over the oil. Season with salt and pepper and bake in the oven for about 20 minutes, until the peppers are tender but not collapsed.

Meanwhile, cook the potatoes in boiling salted water until tender, then drain and mash with 25 g (1 oz) of the butter, the Greek yoghurt and seasoning to taste. Keep warm.

Put half the diced apple in a small bowl, pour over the lemon juice and leave for about 5 minutes, then drain.

Heat half the remaining butter in a small pan, add the onion and fry until softened and brown. Add the bay leaves, sugar and the lemon-soaked apple, season with salt and pepper and cook gently for 5 minutes, until the apple is tender.

Heat the remaining butter in a pan, add the nutmeg, thyme and remaining apple. Cook gently for 5 minutes, until the apple is tender and golden.

Heat the oil in a frying pan and gently fry the black pudding until it has been warmed through.

To serve, put the mashed potato on to 2 warmed serving plates and spoon the apple sauces next to it. Arrange the black pudding on top and accompany with the stuffed peppers.

## BRIAN TURNER

# POTIRON À LA FLAMANDE

Pumpkin stuffed with pork and apple in a cider sauce
*See photograph*

**Looking forward to a Hallowe'en celebration, Linda Walton from West London brought along a pumpkin and some pork. Brian turned the pork into a spooky special and served it inside the pumpkin.**

**SERVES 2**

1 small pumpkin, about 1 kg (2¹/₄ lb)
50 g (2 oz) butter
2 tablespoons vegetable oil
2 eating apples, peeled, cored and finely diced
1 small onion, chopped
350 g (12 oz) potatoes, finely diced
350 g (12 oz) pork loin steak, cut into 5 cm (2 inch) squares

¹/₂ teaspoon paprika
Salt and freshly ground black pepper

**FOR THE SAUCE**
300 ml (10 fl oz) chicken stock
150 ml (5 fl oz) cider
150 ml (5 fl oz) double cream
1 tablespoon Dijon mustard

Pre-heat the oven to gas mark 6, 200°C (400°F).

Slice the top off the pumpkin and scoop out the seeds and most of the flesh, leaving a shell about 1 cm (1/2 inch) thick. Cut half the butter into small pieces and put them in the pumpkin shell. Place the pumpkin in an ovenproof dish and bake in the oven while you prepare the filling.

Heat the remaining butter and half the oil in a frying pan, add the apples, onion and potatoes and cook gently for about 10 minutes, until softened and golden brown. Season to taste. In a separate pan, heat the remaining oil, add the pork and paprika and fry for 8–10 minutes or until cooked through.

To make the sauce, put the stock and cider in a heavy-based pan and boil until reduced to half its original volume. Add the cream and simmer until reduced by almost half again, then stir in the mustard and season to taste.

To serve, stir the apple mixture and the pork into the sauce, then spoon the sauce into the pumpkin, arranging any extra around the pumpkin in the dish.

---

### READY STEADY COOK Tip

*The pumpkin will not be cooked after so short a cooking time. If you have more time, bake it for about 40 minutes or until tender when pierced with a knife. The pumpkin flesh can be diced and cooked in boiling salted water, then stirred into the filling.*

---

## BRIAN TURNER

# AGNEAU AU FER À LA COMPOTE DES FRUITS

Lamb noisettes with fruit compote, runner beans and mint butter sauce

Pete Bowman from Birmingham enjoys lamb but only eats it as the Sunday roast. Brian showed him new ideas for his old favourite by combining it with a fruit compote.

**SERVES 2**

2 x 175 g (6 oz) lamb chump chops
1 tablespoon soy sauce
1 tablespoon runny honey
100 g (4 oz) runner beans, cut into 1 cm (1/2 inch) lengths
15 g (1/2 oz) butter
Salt and freshly ground black pepper

**FOR THE COMPOTE**

1 tablespoon olive oil
1/2 red onion, finely chopped
50 g (2 oz) ready-to-eat dried apricots, roughly chopped
50 g (2 oz) sultanas
125 g (4 oz) cranberries
150 ml (5 fl oz) dry white wine

**FOR THE SAUCE**

300 ml (10 fl oz) chicken stock
150 ml (5 fl oz) dry white wine
4 tablespoons brandy
75 g (3 oz) chilled butter, diced
1 tablespoon finely chopped fresh mint

Cut the lamb off the bone and trim off any excess fat, then tie into rounds (noisettes) with kitchen string (you could ask your butcher to do this). Place under a very hot grill for 1 minute on each side until browned. Put the soy sauce and honey in a small pan and heat gently for 1 minute, until slightly reduced and thickened. Brush this mixture all over the lamb and continue to cook for 4–6 minutes, until cooked and slightly caramelized on the outside and pink in the centre. Transfer to an ovenproof dish and keep warm in a low oven.

Meanwhile, make the compote. Heat the oil in a frying pan, add the onion and cook gently for a few minutes, until softened. Add the remaining ingredients and simmer for 10–15 minutes, until the fruit is soft and pulpy and most of the liquid has evaporated.

For the sauce, put the stock and white wine in a pan and boil for 5 minutes, then add the brandy and boil until the liquid is reduced to two-thirds of its original volume. Whisk in the butter a few pieces at a time, and boil until reduced to about 200 ml (7 fl oz). Stir in the mint and season to taste.

Cook the runner beans in a pan of boiling salted water for 3–4 minutes, until just tender, then drain. Melt the butter in a pan, toss the beans in it and season to taste.

To serve, pile the runner beans in the centre of each serving plate, place the lamb on top and surround with the fruit compote. Pour the sauce around the edge.

## ANTONY WORRALL THOMPSON

# ALISON'S HOT AND SPICY DREAM

### Steak with saffron rice and oyster mushroom stir-fry

*Alison Hannigan from Rayleigh, Essex, had been given a wok but never had the courage to use it — or even get it out of the cupboard! With her favourite Chinese ingredients of beef, beansprouts, mushrooms and ginger, she challenged Antony to create a stir-fry that would inspire her to use the wok at home.*

| SERVES 4 | FOR THE STIR-FRY |
|---|---|
| 175 g (6 oz) easy-cook long grain rice | 1 chicken stock cube |
| A large pinch of saffron strands | 175 g (6 oz) easy-cook long grain rice |
| 1 tablespoon sunflower oil | 100 g (4 oz) frozen peas |
| 350 g (12 oz) sirloin steak | 2 eggs |
| 1 tablespoon chopped fresh coriander | 3 tablespoons sunflower oil |
| | 1 onion, finely chopped |

3 garlic cloves, finely chopped
1 teaspoon ginger purée
1/2 teaspoon hot chilli powder
1 lemon grass stalk, finely chopped
85 ml (3 fl oz) water
100 g (4 oz) oyster mushrooms, sliced

100 g (4 oz) beansprouts
2 tablespoons soy sauce
2 tablespoons chopped fresh coriander
1 tablespoon chopped fresh parsley
Salt and freshly ground black pepper

First start preparing the stir-fry. Bring a pan of water to the boil, crumble in the stock cube and then add the rice. Simmer for 10–12 minutes or until the rice is just tender, adding the peas after about 8 minutes. Drain thoroughly and set aside.

Beat the eggs with 1 tablespoon of cold water and some seasoning. Heat 1 tablespoon of the oil in a 20 cm (8 inch) frying pan, pour in the eggs and cook, stirring the eggs and tilting the pan, to make an omelette. After 2–3 minutes, when the eggs are almost set, cook for a minute longer without stirring, then roll up the omelette, tip out on to a board and leave to cool.

Put the rice and saffron into a pan of boiling salted water and simmer for 10–12 minutes, until tender. Drain and keep warm.

Heat the oil in a griddle or a heavy-based frying pan until very hot. Add the steak and fry for 3–4 minutes on each side.

To finish the stir-fry, heat the remaining oil in a wok until very hot. Add the onion, garlic, ginger purée, chilli powder and lemon grass and stir-fry for 2 minutes. Add the water, then add the mushrooms and beansprouts and stir-fry for 1 minute. Stir in the white rice and peas with the soy sauce, coriander and parsley. Cut the rolled omelette into thin slices and add to the stir-fry.

To serve, spoon the saffron rice around the edge of a serving platter and sprinkle over the coriander. Fill the centre of the plate with the stir-fry. Slice the steak diagonally into strips and arrange on top.

---

### READY STEADY COOK Tip
*Reserve the ends from the onion and add one to each pan of rice for a little extra flavour.*

---

# DESSERTS

SEXY TOFFEE PUDDING AND
HEALTH ON A PLATE – 80

SAGITTARIAN PLUM TARTS WITH
GREEK YOGHURT – 82

CHOCOLATE MOUSSE – 83

ALI'S BIRTHDAY MONTAGE – 84

CARAMELIZED GROUND RICE PUDDINGS ON
A BED OF EXOTIC BANANA – 86

BAKED BANANAS WITH PINEAPPLE CARPACCIO
AND CARAMEL SAUCE – 87

FRUIT HEARTS – 89

PEARS WITH CRANBERRY COMPOTE AND
TWO-CHOCOLATE SAUCE – 90

## ANTONY WORRALL THOMPSON

# SEXY TOFFEE PUDDING AND HEALTH ON A PLATE

### Panettone and banana pudding with pink grapefruit and yoghurt salad

Rita Gordon from Denton, Manchester wanted Antony to make her the ultimate gooey pudding. She brought along a panettone, a reminder of a holiday in Italy with husband Keith.

**SERVES 6**
225 g (8 oz) butter
225 g (8 oz) light soft brown sugar
8 tablespoons golden syrup
5 ripe but firm bananas
450 g (1 lb) panettone, cut horizontally into slices 2 cm (3/4 inch) thick
200 ml (7 fl oz) double cream
150 ml (5 fl oz) milk

**FOR THE PINK GRAPEFRUIT SALAD**
1 pink grapefruit
Juice of 1/2 orange
Grated rind of 1 orange
150 ml (5 fl oz) Greek yoghurt
25 g (1 oz) caster sugar
1 tablespoon finely chopped fresh mint

First make the pink grapefruit salad. Peel the grapefruit, removing all the white pith, and cut out the segments from between the membranes. Squeeze the juice from the grapefruit membranes into a bowl and mix in the orange juice, half the orange rind, the yoghurt, caster sugar and mint. Spoon this mixture on to a serving plate and arrange the grapefruit segments on top, then sprinkle over the remaining orange rind.

Pre-heat the oven to gas mark 8, 230°C (450°F).

Divide the butter, brown sugar and golden syrup between 2 pans, one of which should be large enough to hold 2 whole bananas. Heat gently until the butter has melted and the sugar has dissolved, stirring now and again. Bring to the boil and simmer for about 3 minutes.

Peel the bananas and cut 3 of them into slices 1 cm ($^1/_2$ inch) thick. Add the sliced bananas to one of the pans of toffee sauce. Add the 2 remaining bananas to the other pan of toffee sauce. Continue to simmer both, stirring occasionally, for 3–4 minutes.

Use half the panettone slices to line the base of a 1.7 litre (3 pint) ovenproof dish, cutting them to fit. Put 150 ml (5 fl oz) of the cream in a pan with the milk and heat gently, then pour half of this mixture over the panettone. Spoon over the sliced banana sauce and cover with the remaining panettone. Pour over the remaining cream mixture and spoon over most of the toffee sauce from the second pan, reserving the whole bananas. Put the pudding in the oven for 5 minutes until it is heated through and caramelized on top. If necessary, place it under a hot grill to caramelize.

To serve, arrange the whole bananas on top of the panettone pudding and spoon over any remaining toffee sauce. Pour over the rest of the cream. Serve the pink grapefruit salad separately – or to anyone who is too fainthearted to tackle the pudding!

---

### *READY STEADY COOK Tips*

• *Panettone is a light Italian fruit bread, attractively packaged in boxes and available from delicatessens and supermarkets. If you cannot find one you could substitute brioche or a light fruit loaf.*

• *The pink grapefruit and yoghurt salad makes a refreshing breakfast dish – particularly if you have indulged in toffee pudding the night before!*

• *The toffee and sliced banana sauce makes a superb topping for ice-cream.*

---

## BRIAN TURNER

# SAGITTARIAN PLUM TARTS WITH GREEK YOGHURT

Ann Price from Stratford-upon-Avon is an astrology fan with a sweet tooth. In honour of her star sign, Brian made this fabulously fruity pudding, which tasted out of this world.

**SERVES 4**

175 g (6 oz) strawberry jam
50 g (2 oz) sultanas
100 g (4 oz) seedless black grapes, halved
4 tablespoons damson wine or red wine
A pinch of black pepper
4 tablespoons Greek yoghurt
250 ml (8 fl oz) double cream, lightly whipped
25 g (1 oz) butter

6 plums, halved and stoned
Caster sugar, to taste (optional)
Icing sugar, for dusting

**FOR THE PASTRY**

25 g (1 oz) ground almonds
225 g (8 oz) plain flour
100 g (4 oz) butter, diced
A pinch of salt
1 egg, beaten

Pre-heat the oven to gas mark 6, 200°C (400°F).

First make the pastry. Process the ground almonds, flour, butter and salt in a food processor until combined. Add the egg and process until the mixture just begins to bind together. Add a little cold water if necessary (no more than 1 tablespoon) and process just until the pastry forms a ball around the blade. Chill the pastry for at least 10 minutes, preferably half an hour. Roll out on a lightly floured surface until 5 mm ($1/4$ inch) thick and use to line four 10 cm (4 inch) tart tins. Cover each pastry case with a piece of crumpled greaseproof paper, weighed down with baking beans, and bake for 10 minutes. Remove the paper and baking beans and bake for a further 5 minutes, until the pastry is lightly browned. Remove from the oven and leave to cool on a wire rack.

Put the strawberry jam in a pan and heat, stirring occasionally, until melted. Set aside. Put the sultanas and grapes into a separate pan and heat gently for 1 minute, then add the wine and black pepper. Simmer for 3 minutes, until slightly reduced, then use a slotted spoon to transfer half the mixture to a bowl, draining it well. Leave to cool and then fold in the Greek yoghurt and 4 tablespoons of the whipped cream. Add the jam to the mixture in the pan and simmer until thickened, then remove from the heat and leave to cool.

Melt the butter in a pan, add the plum halves and cook gently for about 5 minutes, until tender. Taste and add a little sugar if necessary. Leave to cool.

Divide the fruit and yoghurt mixture between the pastry cases and place 3 plum halves on top of each one. Pipe the remaining cream on top of each tartlet.

To serve, place each tartlet on a serving plate and spoon the grape and jam compote around them. Dust with icing sugar.

A N T O N Y    W O R R A L L    T H O M P S O N

# CHOCOLATE MOUSSE
*See photograph*

### SERVES 2
100 g (4 oz) good-quality plain chocolate
2 eggs, separated
2 tablespoons double cream
2 tablespoons caster sugar

Break up the chocolate and melt it in a bowl set over a pan of simmering water (make sure the bowl is not touching the water). Remove from the heat and cool slightly, then beat in the egg yolks with a wooden spoon. Stir in the cream.

Whisk the egg whites until they form peaks, then add the sugar and continue to whisk until peaks form again. Using a metal spoon, gently fold the egg whites into the chocolate mixture, then spoon the mousse into individual moulds or dishes and chill for at least 30 minutes, preferably longer, until set.

BRIAN TURNER

# ALI'S BIRTHDAY MONTAGE

As a special treat on her birthday, Ali Stevenson from Nottingham brought along some of her favourite fruits for a summer indulgence. She was delighted to be able to make something in 20 minutes – at home her two small daughters insist on 'mucking in' and everything takes twice as long!

**SERVES 4**

1 plum or peach, stoned and finely diced
1 mango, peeled, stoned and finely diced
50 g (2 oz) cherries, stoned and finely diced
100 g (4 oz) strawberries, sliced
caster sugar, to taste
150 ml (5 fl oz) double cream
icing sugar, for dusting

**FOR THE HAZELNUT BISCUITS**
75 g (3 oz) hazelnuts

75 g (3 oz) self-raising flour
75 g (3 oz) caster sugar
75 g (3 oz) butter
1 egg yolk, lightly beaten

**FOR THE STRAWBERRY COULIS**
225 g (8 oz) strawberries
25 g (1 oz) icing sugar, or to taste
1 tablespoon lemon juice, or to taste

Pre-heat the oven to gas mark 4, 180°C (350°F).

First make the biscuits. Process the hazelnuts finely in a food processor. Add the flour, sugar and butter and continue to process until the mixture resembles fine crumbs. Add the egg yolk and blend briefly. You may not need all the egg yolk; the mixture should just bind together but should not be wet. Form the dough into a log shape about 5 cm (2 inch) in diameter, wrap in greaseproof paper and chill in the freezer until firm.

Cut the biscuit dough into slices about 5 mm ($^1/_4$ inch) thick, place them well spaced out on a greased baking sheet and bake in the oven for 8–10 minutes, until pale golden. Transfer to a wire rack to cool.

For the strawberry coulis, blend the strawberries, icing sugar and lemon juice in a liquidizer until smooth. Pass the coulis through a sieve, then taste and add more icing sugar or lemon juice if necessary.

Mix together the plum or peach, mango, cherries and strawberries and sweeten to taste with caster sugar. Whip the cream until it forms soft peaks.

To serve, sift icing sugar over 4 of the biscuits and set aside. Place a biscuit on each serving plate, top with some of the fruit and then with a little whipped cream. Put another biscuit on top and repeat the fruit and cream layers, then top with the biscuits dusted with icing sugar. Pour the strawberry coulis around the biscuit stacks and serve.

---

### READY STEADY COOK Tips

• *You need 12 biscuits for this recipe so there will be some left over. Either bake all the biscuits and store the extra in an airtight tin, or cut 12 biscuits, then wrap the remaining dough and store in the freezer. When you want to make more biscuits it is very convenient simply to slice off what you need from the frozen dough.*

• *Any soft fruits can be used – try raspberries, blueberries, peaches, kiwi fruit, grapes or melon.*

• *Strawberry coulis goes well with ice-cream, fruit tarts and salads. It will keep in the refrigerator for 2 days and also freezes well.*

---

## BRIAN TURNER

# CARAMELIZED GROUND RICE PUDDINGS ON A BED OF EXOTIC BANANA

Betty Leigh, who runs a Blackpool B&B, gave Brian a real challenge when she brought along some ground rice. Undaunted, he turned it into a winning dish.

| SERVES 4 | FOR THE SAUCE |
|---|---|
| **FOR THE PUDDINGS** | 3 oranges |
| 65 g (2½ oz) dried fruit, such as apricots, prunes and peaches, finely diced | 75 g (3 oz) butter |
| | 75 g (3 oz) soft brown sugar |
| 450 ml (15 fl oz) milk | 3 large bananas, diced |
| 100 g (4 oz) ground rice | 3–4 tablespoons rum, to taste |
| 25 g (1 oz) caster sugar | 2 tablespoons honey |
| 300 ml (10 fl oz) double cream | 1 papaya, peeled, de-seeded and diced |
| 2 egg yolks | |
| 50 g (2 oz) soft brown sugar | |

Pre-heat the oven to gas mark 6, 200°C (400°F).

First make the ground rice puddings. Put the dried fruit into a small bowl, pour over hot water to cover and leave to soak for 5–10 minutes. Drain thoroughly and pat dry. Heat the milk in a pan until almost boiling, then add the ground rice, caster sugar and half the double cream. Bring to the boil, stirring continuously, and cook gently for 2 minutes, then whisk in the egg yolks. Remove from the heat and stir in the dried fruit, then spoon the mixture into 4 greased 7.5 cm (3 inch) ramekin dishes or individual brioche moulds. Place the dishes in a roasting tin containing 2.5 cm (1 inch) of water and bake in the oven for about 5 minutes, until set.

For the sauce, remove the rind from one of the oranges with a zester and set aside. Peel the oranges, removing all the white pith, and cut

out the segments from between the membranes. Set aside. Melt 50 g
(2 oz) of the butter and 50 g (2 oz) of the sugar in a frying pan, add
the diced bananas and rum and let the mixture bubble for 1–2
minutes. Be careful not to overcook the bananas; they should retain
their shape. Stir in the orange rind. In a separate pan, melt the
remaining butter and sugar, stir in the orange segments and honey
and cook until caramelized. Stir in the papaya and heat through
gently.

Run a knife round the edge of each ground rice pudding to loosen it
and turn out on to a baking tray or heatproof plate. Sprinkle the
brown sugar over the top and place under a hot grill until
caramelized. Whip the remaining cream until thick.

To serve, spoon the banana sauce into the centre of 4 serving
plates and place the ground rice puddings on top. Arrange the
caramelized oranges and papaya around the edges. Top the
puddings with the whipped cream.

ANTONY  WORRALL  THOMPSON

# BAKED BANANAS WITH PINEAPPLE CARPACCIO AND CARAMEL SAUCE

*See photograph*

The Tainsh family from Largs, Scotland, are known as the banana family at their local
supermarket. True to form, Barbara brought along a bunch of bananas to challenge Antony —
and learnt how to cut a pineapple.

| **SERVES 4** | 85 ml (3 fl oz) double cream |
|---|---|
| 1 small pineapple | 1 teaspoon whisky, or to taste |
| 1 orange | 25 g (1 oz) good-quality plain |
| 1 lime | chocolate, grated |

87

**FOR THE CARAMEL SAUCE**
100 g (4 oz) caster sugar
120 ml (4 fl oz) water
200 ml (7 fl oz) double cream

**FOR THE BAKED BANANAS**
4 bananas
75 g (3 oz) soft brown sugar
1 teaspoon cinnamon
25 g (1 oz) butter
2 tablespooons whisky

Pre-heat the oven to gas mark 5, 190°C (375°F).

First make the caramel sauce. Put the sugar and water in a small pan and heat gently without stirring until dissolved. Bring to the boil and boil steadily for about 5 minutes, until it has turned a rich, golden caramel colour (watch it carefully to make sure it does not become too dark). Remove from the heat and pour in the cream, holding the pan well away from you in case it splatters. Return to the heat and cook gently, stirring, for 1–2 minutes, until the sauce is smooth. Do not let it boil again.

For the baked bananas, peel the bananas and place in a shallow ovenproof dish. Sprinkle over the brown sugar and cinnamon, dot with the butter and then pour over the whisky. Bake in the oven for 10–15 minutes, until softened.

Meanwhile, peel the pineapple, cut it into wafer-thin slices and arrange on a large serving platter. Peel the orange and lime, removing all the white pith, and cut out the segments from between the membranes. Arrange on top of the pineapple. Whip the cream until it forms peaks, then fold in the whisky.

To serve, place the baked bananas in the centre of the platter, on top of the pineapple, then top with the whipped cream and sprinkle over the grated chocolate. Serve with the caramel sauce.

---

### READY STEADY COOK Tip
*To peel the pineapple neatly, slice off all the skin, then remove the knots by making a small angled cut into the fruit on either side of a row of knots (the knots run in diagonal lines along the pineapple) and lifting them out.*

---

# DESSERTS

ANTONY WORRALL THOMPSON

## FRUIT HEARTS
*See photograph*

Paul Morrison from Teddington, Middlesex, asked Antony to make a Valentine's Day dessert for his sweet-toothed wife, Kristen. Antony obliged with this romantic pudding and found time to make a chocolate mousse as well (see page 83). Meanwhile Kristen was cooking a special meal with Brian (see page 38).

| | |
|---|---|
| **SERVES 2** | 2 passion fruit |
| 450 g (1 lb) puff pastry | Caster sugar, to taste |
| 1 egg yolk, beaten with 1 tablespoon water | 8 strawberries, sliced |
| 1 small mango | Icing sugar, for dusting |
| 150 ml (5 fl oz) double cream | |

Pre-heat the oven to gas mark 6, 200°C (400°F).

Cut the pastry in half and roll out each piece on a lightly floured surface to about 1 cm (½ inch) thick. With a sharp knife, cut out a heart shape from each piece of pastry, about 15 cm (6 inch) long. Place on a baking tray, brush with the beaten egg yolk and bake for about 15–20 minutes, until well risen and golden brown. Remove from the oven and leave on a wire rack until cool enough to handle, then cut each heart horizontally in half. If the pastry is not quite cooked through, return the hearts to the oven, cut-side up, for a few minutes. Leave on a wire rack to cool completely.

Meanwhile, peel the mango and cut the flesh away from the stone. Cut a few long slices for decoration and dice the remaining flesh. Set aside.

Whip the cream until thick. Cut the passion fruit in half and use a teaspoon to scoop out the seeds and flesh. Fold them gently into the whipped cream and sweeten to taste with caster sugar.

To serve, place the bottom half of each pastry heart on a serving plate and spread the passion fruit cream over it. Cover the cream with the diced mango and strawberries and top with the remaining pastry half. Dust the fruit hearts with icing sugar and decorate with the reserved mango slices.

---

**READY STEADY COOK Tip**
*To make 2 pastry hearts exactly the same size, cut out one heart, then place it on the other piece of pastry and cut round it. Alternatively you could use a cardboard template.*

---

BRIAN TURNER

# PEARS WITH CRANBERRY COMPOTE AND TWO-CHOCOLATE SAUCE

*See photograph*

Stephanie Bayliss from Beckenham, Kent, confessed to having a very sweet tooth. She brought along two types of chocolate and some fruit and Brian put together this luxurious dessert.

| | |
|---|---|
| **SERVES 2** | **FOR THE COMPOTE** |
| 2 pears | 25 g (1 oz) butter |
| Juice of $\frac{1}{2}$ lemon | 50 g (2 oz) caster sugar |
| Grated rind of 1 orange | 225 g (8 oz) cranberries |
| 25 g (1 oz) butter | Juice of $\frac{1}{2}$ orange |
| A little caster sugar, for sprinkling | **FOR THE CHOCOLATE SAUCE** |
| 2 ginger nut biscuits, crushed | 150 ml (5 fl oz) double cream |
| 1 tablespoon flaked almonds, toasted | 75 g (3 oz) good-quality plain chocolate |
| Icing sugar, for dusting | 15 g ($\frac{1}{2}$ oz) butter |
| | 25 g (1 oz) white chocolate drops |

First make the cranberry compote. Melt the butter and sugar in a frying pan, add the cranberries and orange juice and simmer for 2 minutes or until softened. Keep warm.

Peel, halve and core the pears, then put them into a bowl of water with the lemon juice to prevent them browning.

Bring a pan of water to the boil, add the orange rind and simmer for 1–2 minutes. Remove with a slotted spoon, refresh in cold water and pat dry. Reserve for decoration. Add the pear halves to the pan and poach for about 5 minutes or until just tender. Drain the pear halves, then place them on a board, cut-side down, and slice thinly, leaving them joined at the top. Press down lightly on each pear half with the palm of your hand to make a fan shape. Melt the butter in a frying pan and, using a fish slice, carefully transfer the pears to it, rounded-side down. Fry until golden, then turn over to cook the other side. Sprinkle with a little caster sugar and place under a hot grill until lightly caramelized. Keep warm.

To make the chocolate sauce, bring the double cream to the boil in a pan, then gradually add chunks of the plain chocolate, whisking until smooth. Remove from the heat and whisk in the butter to give a glossy finish.

To serve, spoon the cranberry compote into the centre of 2 large serving plates and arrange the pears on top. Sprinkle with the orange rind and the crushed ginger nut biscuits. Pour the hot chocolate sauce around and dot the white chocolate drops all over it – they will melt into the sauce. Finally sprinkle over the flaked almonds and dust with icing sugar.

---

### READY STEADY COOK Tip
*This is delicious but extremely rich. For a simpler dessert, just serve the pears on the cranberry compote, sprinkled with the flaked almonds and dusted with icing sugar. You could just poach the pears, omitting the caramelizing. The chocolate sauce is very good with ice-cream.*

---

# READY STEADY COOK

## INDEX

### A

apples
pumpkin stuffed with pork and
apple in a cider sauce 74–5
spicy mackerel fillets on tasty
Tenby treats 27–8
asparagus 38–9
aubergines 14
and tomato sauce 10

### B

bacon
bacon–wrapped tomatoes 57–8
fried kidneys and bacon on carrot
purée with mushroom and
coriander sauce 62–3
bananas
baked with pineapple carpaccio
and caramel sauce 87–8
banana sauce 86–7
deep–fried 47–8
panettone and banana pudding
80–1
beans see green beans; haricot
beans; runner beans
beef
jet–lag steak stack 63–4
meatballs with couscous,
vegetables and mint and
yoghurt sauce 65–6
spaghetti bolognese 70
spicy steak with warm mushroom

salad and hollandaise sauce
59–60
steak and ratatouille with polenta
and grilled vegetables 67–8
steak with saffon rice and oyster
mushroom stir–fry 77–8
biscuits, hazelnut 84–5
black pudding à la forestière with
Piedmontese peppers 73–4
brandy cream sauce 22–3
brioche, baked filled with pork and
sage patties, mushrooms, bacon–
wrapped tomatoes, fried eggs
and fried onion rings 57–8
bruschetta with olive paste,
aubergine and Mozzarella 14
bubble and squeak, Yorkshire 42–3

### C

cabbage 69
parcels 16–7
caramel sauce 87–8
carrots
and leek garnish 29–30
purée 62–3
rösti 43–4
celeriac, roasted 49–50
cheeses see red Leicester;
Mozzarella; ricotta
chick pea salad 54–5
chicken
Atlanta with kumquat chutney and
asparagus 38–9
breasts and tomatoes stuffed with

92